Irina Wiegand

The Protection of Human Rights and Fundamental Freedoms in the Fight against Terrorism

The Case of the European Union after September 11, 2001

Irina Wiegand

THE PROTECTION OF HUMAN RIGHTS AND FUNDAMENTAL FREEDOMS IN THE FIGHT AGAINST TERRORISM

The Case of the European Union after September 11, 2001

ibidem-Verlag
Stuttgart

Bibliografische Information der Deutschen Nationalbibliothek
Die Deutsche Nationalbibliothek verzeichnet diese Publikation in der Deutschen Nationalbibliografie; detaillierte bibliografische Daten sind im Internet über http://dnb.d-nb.de abrufbar.

Bibliographic information published by the Deutsche Nationalbibliothek
Die Deutsche Nationalbibliothek lists this publication in the Deutsche Nationalbibliografie; detailed bibliographic data are available in the Internet at http://dnb.d-nb.de.

∞

Gedruckt auf alterungsbeständigem, säurefreien Papier
Printed on acid-free paper

ISBN-10: 3-89821-894-5

ISBN-13: 978-3-89821-894-8

Printed in Germany

Acknowledgements

I wish to thank Prof. Dr. Dr. Dr. h.c. mult. Georg Ress and Prof. Dr. Margrit Schreier for their extremely helpful suggestions, feedbacks and comments and for encouraging me to continue with this research. I would like to express my appreciation for the incredible degree of support that they offered me.

I would also like to thank all those who commented on my draft. Special thanks in this respect are due to Liuben Siarov for providing me with helpful comments throughout the whole process of writing this book.

Finally, I owe thanks to Andrew James Klassen for revising and proofreading the final text and to Michal Onderco for helping me to do the final editorial work.

Bremen, March 2008 Irina Wiegand

Contents

List of Abbreviations

BR	*Brigate Rosse* / Red Brigades
CFR-CDF	EU Network of Independent Experts in Human Rights
EAW	European Arrest Warrant
EC	European Community
ECHR	European Convention for the Protection of Human Rights and Fundamental Freedoms
ECJ	Court of Justice of the European Communities / European Court of Justice
ECrtHR	European Court of Human Rights
ETA	*Euskadi Ta Askatasuna* / Basque Homeland and Freedom
EU	European Union
Europol	European Police Office
FRONTEX	European Agency for the Management of Operational Cooperation at the External Borders
ICCL	Irish Council for Civil Liberties
ICCPR	International Covenant on Civil and Political Rights
ICJ	International Commission of Jurists
ICrtJ	International Court of Justice
ILC	International Law Commission
IRA	Irish Republican Army
JHA	Justice and Home Affairs
KFOR	Kosovo Force
NATO	North Atlantic Treaty Organization
NGO	Non-Governmental Organization
OHCHR	Office of the High Commissioner for Human Rights
PKK	*Partiya Karkerên Kurdistan* / Kurdistan Workers Party
PLO	Palestine Liberation Organization / *Munazzamat at-Tahrīr al-Filastīniyya*
PNR	Passenger Name Record
RAF	*Rote Armee Fraktion* / Red Army Fraction
SC	Security Council
TEU	Treaty on European Union, Maastricht Treaty
UDHR	Universal Declaration of Human Rights
UN	United Nations
UNC	Charter of the United Nations
UNMIK	United Nations Mission in Kosovo
UNSC	United Nations Security Council
US	United States (of America)
9/11	Terrorist attacks in the US on September 11, 2001

"The present situation shows that, for all of us, but especially for the U.S. and Europe, security in the 21st century can no longer be defined by the traditional categories of the 20th century.
A new totalitarianism, Islamist terrorism and its inhumane Jihad ideology, pose a threat to peace and stability, both regionally and globally[1]."

Introduction

Germany's former Foreign Minister, JOSCHKA FISCHER, started a speech at the University of Princeton in 2003 with these words. Individual states are no longer able to counter the threat of terrorism and multilateral cooperation – on the EU level, but also trans-Atlantic and global cooperation – is needed to combat terrorism effectively. Spreading knowledge about and insisting on respect for fundamental values, in particular human rights, is of major importance in this cooperation aimed at fighting the threat of terrorism (FISCHER 2003).
Certainly, terrorism is not a new phenomenon: In the EU, terrorism has existed for decades and still does.. For example the Federal Republic of Germany and Italy were confronted with leftist terrorist movements, such as the RAF or the BR during the 1970s, while other parts of Europe have had to struggle with terrorist independence movements, such as the IRA or, in Spain, the ETA.
As long as these different terrorist groups have acted, the individual states have countered the threat resulting from their action. With respect to countermeasures, it has sometimes been claimed that states violate human rights. In the case of the Federal Republic of Germany for example, changes in the code of procedure were introduced as an anti-terrorist measure, in order to restrict the rights of the accused terrorists in their trial. Another example is solitary confinement of RAF terrorists, in the so-called dead wings of Germany's prisons. Already in 1977, Amnesty International Germany expressed its deep concern about the curtailing of human rights in the fight against terrorism. Especially the imprisonment in complete isolation has been considered as a method of torture.
Terrorism, the fight against it and claims about human rights violations in this fight are thus not new in Europe. But whereas the terrorists' goals were predominantly regional in scope in the past, the situation is different today.

With the terrorist attacks on the Twin Towers of New York's World Trade Center in September 2001, the terrorist threat has changed considerably. This event, where Islamic extremists hijacked four commercial passenger airplanes and intentionally crashed two of them into the World Trade center's Twin Towers, a third one into the Pentagon and the fourth failed and crashed in a field, has marked the beginning of the realization – and perhaps the practice – of a dimension of terrorism that can constitute a considerable threat on a global level. In the aftermath of these devastating attacks, European countries have also fallen victim to this 'new' form of terrorism, for example in March 2004 attacks on Madrid's commuter trains took place and in July 2005 a coordinated suicide bombing on several underground trains and busses took place in London.

Due to this internationality of terrorism, states are in need of more effective models for preventive actions and countermeasures to the increased threat of terrorist attacks. And, to come back to Joschka Fischer's speech, in order to be effective, the states have to act jointly. Within the framework of the EU, this has indeed increasingly happened. Cooperation had already begun long before 2001, but since 9/11, the EU has – based on the Treaty of Amsterdam – expanded its common anti-terrorism law and policies internally as well as on the international level (MONAR 2005b:425).

But howsoever the fight against terrorism is organized, it poses a challenge to the international community, insofar as the community has to "defend itself against the dangers of terrorism" (AREND and HEINZ 2005:5) while respecting its own values, such as human rights norms, that terrorists "aim to destroy" (ANNAN 2003). "Respect for human rights, fundamental freedoms and the rule of law" (ibid) should be essential in the effort to combat terrorism.

But if some European states have combated terrorism in the past by violating human rights and limiting civil liberties – at a time when the threat to international peace and security was far less than it is today – it might be that they now react in a similar way. The fact that the ICJ (2005:351) states in its 2004 adopted 'Declaration on upholding Human Rights and the Rule of Law in Combating Terrorism': "Terrorism poses a serious threat to human rights. (..) Since September 2001 many states have adopted new counter-terrorism measures that are in breach of their international obligations", seems to indicate this and indeed, especially fundamental rights, such as the right to

[1] Germany's former Foreign Minister, JOSCHKA FISCHER, in a speech on November 19, 2003 at Princeton University.

privacy, are touched in the EU by some of the measures enacted in order to fight terrorism.

Whereas a lot is known about the practice of the US and their 'war on terrorism', less is known in the wider public about measures of the EU in order to counter the terrorist threat. This is on the one hand surprising, as the EC member states had already started cooperation with regard to terrorism in the 1970s; on the other hand, it is not surprising, because the fight against terrorism is anchored in the field of internal security – an area where the member states want to preserve as much sovereignty as they can. For this reason, the EU has only limited competencies. But it still has some scope of action and it has made use of it and agreed on a number of legislative measures.

In this book, I will mainly look at the EU reactions to terrorism after September 11, 2001, with special focus on the protection of human rights. The research question to be answered is thus:

How has the EU reacted to the 'new' threat of global terrorism and how do these post-9/11 reactions on terrorism relate to the law of human rights and fundamental freedoms?

Pursuing this research question and the topic in general bear significant value, as this constitutes an up-to-date issue and a matter of considerable debate. For example, there are severe controversies regarding the question of whether inhuman treatment of suspects of terrorism can be justified in the fight against terrorism or not. As the debate is a contemporary one, there are many recent publications on the topic, including books, journal articles but also newspaper articles. Different works evaluate the EU's fight against terrorism and the compatibility of security and freedom or civil rights[2]. Books focusing on human rights in the Bush administration's 'war on terror' have also been published[3], elaborating on questions such as whether human rights should be or are still universal in an age of global terrorism. This book will be a contribution to this ongoing debate.

[2] See for example KAHL (2006) or MÜLLER and SCHNEIDER (2006).
[3] See for example WILSON (2005).

Research Design and Structure

This book will focus on legislative measures adopted on the EU level and their relation to the law of fundamental rights. For this reason, the underlying research design is that of a single case study. As the individual member states are not the units of analysis, the case study is holistic.

The research question to be answered basically consists of two parts, which are both descriptive: first the main legislative measures that have been adopted by the EU will be identified and in a second step, those measures that might be questionable from a human rights perspective will be evaluated in the light of existing human rights law.

Due to the nature of the topic, it is necessary to work with both primary and secondary sources. For those parts, explaining international law, mainly primary sources will be used, such as conventions, treaties or UN resolutions. For the part about the EU's actions, both primary sources, such as official EU or governmental documents, and secondary sources, like analytical books or articles will be used.

My analysis can lead to basically two different conclusions:

a) the EU complies with fundamental human rights law in their actions; or

b) the EU does not comply with human rights law in certain respects.

In order to give a comprehensive answer to my research question, the book will start with a chapter providing the necessary background information for dealing with the topic, namely what is terrorism, who is Al Qaeda and what is the legal framework for states being attacked by terrorist organizations?

This introductory part is important, because it is necessary to have a certain basic knowledge of terrorism and terrorist organizations in order to understand the states' reactions to the terrorist threat.

In the first sub-chapter "The Phenomenon of Terrorism and International Law" a brief description of terrorism and its relation to international law will be given, this includes a brief look at the historical roots of terrorism and the legal framework with regard to terrorism in Europe.

In the second introductory chapter, terrorist organizations will be dealt with. The chapter will essentially focus on Al Qaeda, as this network has been made responsible for the attacks on 9/11 and a number of other terrorist acts. Today's fight against terrorism is mainly focused on the Al Qaeda network.

The third introductory part will deal with the challenges that terrorism poses to international law, which is essentially inter-state law. But one of the main global threats today comes from a terrorist, non-state organization. What does this mean for a state's right of self-defense? This is the main question that will be answered in this part, which is important, because the EU has supported the US by invading Afghanistan in the aftermath of 9/11.

Having given this background information, the second chapter will focus on the European reactions to terrorism. It will start with a general overview of EU reactions to terrorism. As terrorism is not a new phenomenon in the European states, cooperation in the fight against it started decades ago, namely in the 1970s. The overview will begin with the conventions and measures adopted between this time and 9/11. In addition, the EU was founded during that time and the relevant legal framework for EU action was established. Basic information in this regard will also be given in this chapter. However, the main focus will be on the reactions after September 11, 2001 and the terrorist bombings in Madrid, in March 2004, and in London, in July 2005, in order to show how far these events have influenced the EU in the fight against terrorism. It is not possible to summarize and describe all measures decided and enacted in the fight against terrorism – more than 200 individual measures have been adopted since September 2001 –, therefore only the main reactions will be summarized, with a focus on those that might be questionable from a human rights perspective.

This part will be followed by a chapter about the law of human and fundamental rights in the EU, in order to provide the necessary background information for an evaluation of those EU reactions that might violate fundamental rights. In a first step, some basic information on human rights law on the international level will be given, by briefly looking at the main Declarations and Covenants of the UN, namely the 'Universal Declaration on Human Rights', the 'International Covenant of Civil and Political Rights' and the 'International Covenant of Economic, Social and Cultural Rights'. In a second part, I will turn to regional human rights law, by having a closer look at the 'European Convention for the Protection of Human Rights and Fundamental Freedoms' and the 'Charter of Fundamental Rights of the European Union'.

Having given this legal background, each of the measures and reactions that might be questionable from a human rights point of view will, in a fourth chapter, be described in a more detailed way and be assessed in the light of human rights law. In this part, the implementation of these measures in national law might serve as examples. Furthermore, relevant judgments of the Court of Justice of the European Communities, of the Court of First Instance and the European Court of Human Rights will be taken into consideration. The book will finish with a conclusion, providing an answer to the research question.

1. Legal Background on Terrorism

The main aim of this book is to look at the EU's reactions to terrorism after the events of 9/11 and to assess whether these reactions respect existing human rights law. However, before coming to the EU's legislative measures and the human rights regime, some general background information is necessary. This will be provided in the following chapters. In a first step, the phenomenon of terrorism will be presented, including a brief look at the history of terrorism, terrorism and international law and finally the notion of terrorism in Europe. This includes the Council of Europe as well as the EU.

In a second step, terrorist organizations will be dealt with, by defining the concept and by looking in more detail to Al Qaeda, which is considered to be today's most dangerous terrorist network.

In a last part, information about terrorism as a challenge to international law will be given. The general prohibition of the use of force on the international level will briefly be presented, before one of the exceptions to this general prohibition, namely the right to self-defense, will be explained. The terrorist threat challenges international law and the right to self-defense insofar as international law traditionally is inter-state law. A brief look at the modification of addressees of defense – namely from states to international criminal organizations – will show how international law has reacted to this changing environment and in which legal framework states can react to the terrorist threat.

1.1 The Phenomenon of Terrorism

Despite the fact that the term 'terrorism' is an old and history-laden expression which is used widely and in different languages, only few other words "are plagued by so much indeterminacy, subjectivity and political disagreement as 'terror', terrorize', 'terrorism' and 'terrorist'" (SAUL 2006:1): Neither in legal terms, nor from a social science point of view, does a clear-cut definition of 'terrorism' exist, even though the international community under the auspices of the League of Nations and the UN, as well as academics have sought a definition for decades already.

In this chapter, I will shed some light on terrorism in more practical terms, that is what kinds of events have been called 'terrorist acts' in the past and today. I will further look at terrorism from a legal point of view, first with regard to international law and then to European law.[4]

1.1.1 The Phenomenon of Terrorism – a brief historical Outline

The term 'terror' was first used in connection with the '*Regime de la Terreur'* – 'Reign of Terror', in the aftermath of the French Revolution, when thousands of people were executed (HOFFMAN 2001:17; MURPHY 1989:14). Thus, contrary to today, when terrorism is mostly associated with non-state actors, it was first an instrument of state control. Other examples for the use of terror in this relation are the German Nazi-Regime or the Stalinist regime in Russia.

It was only in the late nineteenth century that terrorism slowly became associated with non-state groups, like revolutionaries in the tsarist Russia. Examples for this kind of terrorist acts are the assassination of Tsar Alexander II of Russia in 1881 or the assassination of Archduke Franz Ferdinand in 1914 (HOFFMAN 2001:20-24). At this time, terrorist acts were usually targeted assassinations, and the terrorists tried to avoid the killing of innocent people. This is a major difference to the forms of terrorism that emerged after World War II, because these new formations have usually accepted the killing of innocents.

After the Second World War, the term underwent another change of meaning: it was often linked to independence movements fighting against colonization. It was at this time, that the term 'freedom fighters' was also used in relation to terrorists for the first time (ibid:30). One example for this is the PLO.

During the 1960s and 1970s the term was used even more broadly, when applying it to separatist groups in the western world, such as the ETA in Spain. It was also at that time that left-extremist groups, like the RAF in the Federal Republic Germany or the BR in Italy, which fought against the capitalistic society in Western Europe, were called terrorists.

In the late twentieth century, after the end of the Cold War, a new form of fundamentalist religious terrorism has emerged. The best-known terrorist organization for this period is Al Qaeda, which has been made responsible for the

[4] For more sociological approaches see for example SCHMID (2004), who has derived at ten different elements of terrorism or FLETCHER (2006), who identifies eight variables. Both arrived at their elements from evaluating different existing definitions of terrorism.

terrorist attacks on New York's World Trade Center on September 11, 2001, but also for other attacks, like those on trains and busses in Madrid in 2004 (SAUL 2006:2-3). What is important about this new form of terrorism is that it has become globalized, terrorists are able to inflict extreme high damages upon the affected population, it has been realized that terrorist acts are not very expensive[5] and that the aims of those terrorist organizations are not clear (MAHNCKE 2006:19). Another characteristic is the central role of mass media: terrorists today know how to exploit the global media in order to spread their propaganda. One has just to think of 9/11, which was broadcasted live all over the world; most probably the effect of these attacks would have been less without the mass media.

This brief historical outline shows that the term terrorism has been used for a range of different acts over the last decades. While there is today some broad agreement that the essence of terrorism is that it "denotes unlawful violence by non-state actors directed against non-military targets for political purposes" (NEUHOLD 2006:23), it is difficult to give one precise and exact definition. This results partly from the whole range of different events that have been called terrorist acts. Another problem of definition "lies in the risk it entails of taking positions" (ZEIDAN 2004:491). Here the problem that 'one man's terrorist is another man's freedom fighter' becomes obvious, because so far, attempts to define terrorism have not been merely legally, but also politically motivated (LAVALLE 2007:90[6]). As a result, there are many different, even contradicting, definitions[7] and "the term terrorism has become so widely used in many contexts as to become almost meaningless." (RICHARDSON 2000:209).

---

[5] The estimated costs for 9/11 amount to 500000€ and for the Madrid attacks only to 25000€, which is relatively cheap, especially if compared to the costs of anti-terrorist measures. See for example MAHNCKE (2006).

[6] LAVALLE argues that this politicization is one problem why there is a lack of definition and that a legal definition should be aimed at. See LAVALLE (2007) for more information on the definitional problem of terrorism.

[7] See for example MALLOY (2004), who has made a brief survey of more than 330 provisions of US federal law touching upon terrorism and found that the term is defined in quite different, even competing ways. Partly, even within the same acts, i.e. the Homeland Security Act, terrorism is defined differently and contradictorily in different sections (MALLOY 2004: 39-41). See also SCHMID (2004), who gives four different definitions by United States government agencies.

1.1.2 Terrorism and International Law

As the term terrorism is used not only in the wider public, but also by governments or international organizations, a clear definition is needed. Otherwise, international cooperation in the fight against international terrorism becomes almost impossible and meaningless, because if countries do not agree on what terrorism is, it is rather unlikely that it can effectively be fought (GANOR 1998; SCHMID 2004:380). Furthermore, the term is used in different UN resolutions and therefore has legal consequences for the member states. For this and several other reasons, most academics and the international community agree that an "I know it, when I see it" approach (DUGARD 2005:187) is not sufficient. It is therefore not surprising that the international community has been working on a definition since the 1920s already. Several international conventions dealing with terrorism have been adopted since then.

Before the Second World War, the League of Nations had already worked on a Convention: in 1937, the 'Convention for the Prevention and Punishment of Terrorism' was adopted, but it never came into force, mainly because of the rejection by Great Britain and Nazi-Germany (SAUL 2005:59-63; WOIT 2004:143). Article 1 of this convention

> "defines 'acts of terrorism' as 'criminal acts directed against a State and intended or calculated to create a state of terror in the minds of particular persons, or a group of persons or the general public'" (MURPHY 1989:15).

This and also the following definitions often refer to the "state of terror". State of terror does not have a special definition; it rather refers to a situation of general fear and anxiety (DENNINGER 2002:29).

After the Second World War when the UN was established, they did not continue the work on this Convention and it was only in 1972, after the terrorist attack at the Olympic Games in Munich, that the UN started the debate on a comprehensive convention on terrorism[8]. In the same year, the General Assembly passed a resolution called 'Measures to prevent international terrorism which endangers or takes innocent

---

[8] This does not mean that terrorism and its definition were not debated between the end of the Second World War and the Munich terrorist attacks in 1972. For example in the 1950s, the ILC worked on a Draft Code. See SAUL (2005) for further information.

human lives or jeopardizes fundamental freedoms, and study of the underlying causes of those forms of terrorism and acts of violence which lie in misery, frustration, grievance and despair, and which cause some people to sacrifice human lives, including their own, in an attempt to effect radical changes' (United Nations 1987). An Ad Hoc Committee on International Terrorism and several sub-committees were established, but no consensus on a definition could be achieved.

Thenceforward, no further attempts for a general definition had been made until the end of the Cold War and the UN was more concerned with specific elements of terrorism (GOLDER and WILLIAMS 2004:274).

In 1994, the UN Declaration on 'Measures to Eliminate International Terrorism' was adopted, which declares "all acts, methods and practices of terrorism as criminal and unjustifiable, wherever and by whomever committed". It does, however, not define the term. Two years later, the Ad hoc Committee established by the General Assembly Resolution 51/210 started its work, *inter alia*, on a Comprehensive Convention against International Terrorism. The 'International Convention for the Suppression of Terrorist Bombings' (1998) and the 'International Convention for the Suppression of the Financing of Terrorism' (1999) have been elaborated by this Committee, but no Comprehensive Convention could be reached (United Nations 1996, 2007a).

After the terrorist attack on the World Trade Center in September 2001, the international community was closer to a definition than ever, but the countries could still not agree on some details. The two most contentious elements until today have been whether national liberation movements should be exempted from terrorism and whether the term should apply to individuals and groups only or also to states (SCHMID 2004:389).

As mentioned above, the UN did establish rules of international law with regard to specific terrorist acts (SHAW 2003:1049). Until today, at least thirteen treaties dealing with specific issues of terrorism have been adopted. As a result of these different conventions, unlawful acts of hijacking, of hostage taking, of terrorist bombing, of financing terrorist organizations, the use of nuclear material, aviation sabotage, violence at airports, endangering the safety of maritime navigation and the

safety of fixed platforms on the continental shelf and crimes against internationally protected persons are criminalized by the international community[9].
Most of these conventions contain international obligations and "the automatic incorporation of such offences within all extradition agreements" (ibid). Any of these acts, covered by the conventions, is terrorism under international law, if they take place in peacetime (SCHMID 2004:391). Thus, terrorism has been defined in a way that is "specific to the subject-matter of the particular convention" (SOREL 2003:365). Whereas in peacetime these different terrorist attacks are regulated by these conventions and criminal law applies, this is different during wartime. *Durante bello*, terrorist acts are regulated in the 1949 Geneva Conventions and its Additional Protocols[10]. This difference basically results from the fact that in wartime acts are allowed that are forbidden in peacetime and the problem of terrorism is a different one (CUMIN 2004:21).
But coming back to the UN Conventions, even though they can partly serve as a definition of terrorism, there are still gaps, which should be filled. One example for such a gap is that "assassinations of businessmen, engineers, journalists and educators are not covered, while similar acts against diplomats and public officials are prohibited" (SCHARF 2004:365).
In 2004, other attempts have been made to solve the definitional problem of the term, when the UNSC enacted Resolution 1566 under Chapter VII of the UN Charter. In this Resolution, the SC

> "(*r*)*ecalls* that criminal acts, including against civilians, committed with the intent to cause death or serious bodily injury, or taking of hostages, with the purpose to provoke a state of terror in the general public or in a group of persons or particular persons, intimidate a population or compel a government or an international organization to do or abstain from doing any act, which constitute offences within the scope of and as defined in the international conventions and protocols relating to terrorism, are under no circumstances justifiable by considerations of a political, philosophical, racial, ethnic, religious or other similar nature (..)" (United Nations 2004a).

[9] See Appendix I for a list of the thirteen Conventions.
[10] Most notably, the IV Geneva Convention (Article 33) and the two 1977 Additional Protocols (Article 51 of Additional Protocol I and Articles 3 and 14 of Additional Protocol II) refer to terrorism, by prohibiting acts of violence, which breach the principles of military necessity, proportionality and distinction, but by aiming at spreading fear among the population (ARNOLD 2006:300). For further information see ARNOLD (2006) or CUMIN (2004).

In the same year, the UN High-level Panel on Threats, Challenges and Change also suggested a definition of terrorism, which reads as follows:

> "Any action, in addition to action already specified by the existing conventions on aspects of terrorism, the Geneva Conventions and Security Council Resolution 1566 (2004), that is intended to cause death or serious bodily harm to civilians or non-combatants, when the purpose of such act, by its nature or context, is to intimidate a population, or to compel a Government or an international organization to do or to abstain from doing any act" (United Nations 2004b:52).

The CLUB OF MADRID (2005) has recommended the adoption of the above cited definition by the High-level Panel and the conclusion of the 'Comprehensive Convention on International Terrorism', but so far neither the definition nor the convention have been adopted: "After thirty years of hard labor there is still no generally agreed definition of terrorism" (LAQUEUR 2003:232).

1.1.3 The Notion of Terrorism in Europe

Different conventions have been adopted on a regional level. One of the earliest regional conventions is the 'European Convention on the Suppression of Terrorism', which was adopted in 1977 (Council of Europe 1977). This treaty mainly resulted from the different terrorist groups acting in Europe during the 1970s (SAUL 2006:147). One of its primary aims was to facilitate the extradition of terrorists. In 2003, a protocol amending the Convention was adopted, which basically led to the incorporation of the different UN Conventions on terrorism that had been passed since 1977[11] (Council of Europe 2003a).

In 2005, the 'Council of Europe Convention on Laundering, Search, Seizure and Confiscation of the Proceeds from Crime and on Financing Terrorism' was adopted in order to come to terms with the problem of financing terrorism (Council of Europe 2005b).

These different Council of Europe conventions have facilitated cooperation in the fight against terrorism, without trying to define the term.

Also in 2005, the 'Council of Europe Convention on the Prevention of Terrorism' was passed, which basically contains regulations about the prevention of terrorism, the compensation for victims, as well as imposing a duty to investigate offences and to extradite or prosecute the responsible actors. It further requires the states to respect human rights in the implementation of the convention. But the Convention also makes an attempt to define 'acts of terrorism' in the Preamble:

> "Recalling that acts of terrorism have the purpose by their nature and context to seriously intimidate a population or unduly compel a government or an international organization to perform or abstain from performing any act or to seriously destabilize or destroy the fundamental political, constitutional, economic or social structures of a country or an international organization" (Council of Europe 2005a).

This attempt to define terrorism is very similar to the one of the UN High level Panel on the international level. It summarizes the most important elements of a terrorist act, without being too detailed.

In addition to these Council of Europe Conventions, the EU adopted Framework Decisions related to terrorism, the most important of which is the 'Framework Decision on combating terrorism'. The core of this Framework Decision is a definition of terrorism, which basically incorporates the by then existing twelve UN Conventions dealing with terrorism, but goes further and closes some of the above mentioned gaps. It gives a relatively broad definition of terrorism, which reads as follows

> "Each member state shall take the necessary measures to ensure that the intentional acts referred to below in point (a) to (i), as defined as offences under national law, which, given their nature or context, may seriously damage a country or an international organization where committed with the aim of:
>
> - Seriously intimidating a population, or
> - Unduly compelling a Government or international organization to perform or abstain from performing any act, or
> - Seriously destabilizing or destroying the fundamental political, constitutional, economic or social structures of a country or an international organization, shall be deemed to be terrorist offences:
>
> (a) attacks upon a person's life which may cause death;
> (b) attacks upon the physical integrity of a person;
> (c) kidnapping or hostage taking;
> (d) causing extensive destruction to a Government or public facility, a transport system, an infrastructure facility, including an information system, a fixed platform located on the continental shelf, a public place or private property likely to endanger human life or result in major economic loss;
> (e) seizure of aircraft, ships, or other means of public or goods transport;
> (f) manufacture, possession, acquisition, transport, supply or use of weapons, explosives or of nuclear, biological or chemical weapons;

[11] See Appendix I for a list of the UN Conventions on terrorism.

(g) release of dangerous substances, or causing fires, floods or explosions the effect of which is to endanger human life;
(h) interfering with or disrupting the supply of water, power or any other fundamental natural resource the effect of which is to endanger human life;
(i) threatening to commit any of the acts listed in (a) to (h)"
(Council of the European Union 2002a).

This definition was criticized by academics as well as NGOs, such as Statewatch, for being too vague and broad and for not meeting the standards of Article 7 ECHR, no punishment without law and Article 11 ECHR, the freedom of assembly. The problem with this kind of broad and vague definition is that it can be abused and in this way serve to expand executive and police powers without clear limits (BROOMHALL 2004:429). In Chapter 4.1, I will look in more detail at this definition and evaluate it with regard to the human rights concerns that have been raised.

1.1.4 Summary

The main finding of this sub-chapter is that neither on the international, nor on the regional level, does a precise definition of terrorism exist. By having given some of the events called 'terrorist attacks' and some of the attempts to define the phenomenon from the international as well as the regional level, it has become clear why the term is so difficult to define.

Despite the lack of one clear definition, some basic elements of a terrorist act can be identified from the different definitions. These elements can serve as a kind of brief 'working definition' for this paper. It does not contradict the EU definition, but is shorter and summarizes the main and most important components.

Most generally, a terrorist act is "shocking and unpredictable" (DIMITRIJEVIC 2003:603). It is a criminal act, leading to death or serious bodily harm of at least one person, but it can also be damage of public or private property. This action intimidates a certain population group or even the whole population of a country. It aims at influencing the political and organizational decision-making or at destabilizing the structures of a country or an international organization. The justification of the activities does not play a role. Even when they are legitimate, the end does by no means justify such means (TOMUSCHAT 2004:121).

There are basically two main reasons why the international community could so far not agree on a more precise definition: the question of whether the term should apply to non-state actors only or also include states, and the question of whether national liberation movements should be included in the definition or not. In general, the first problem can be ignored in the context of this research, because only non-state actors can fall victim to human rights violations. The second problem has actually not been solved with the EU definition, because it does not explicitly include or exclude national liberation movements and therefore kind of circumvents the problem with its vague wording, and several objections have been made from a human rights perspective precisely because of this vague and unclear wording of the whole definition, which will be discussed in more detail in Chapter 4.1.

1.2 Terrorist Organizations

Acts that are nowadays identified as 'terrorist acts', are usually planned, organized and financed by terrorist groups. A 'terrorist group' is, according to Article 2 of the 'European Framework Decision on Combating Terrorism'

> "a structured group of more than two persons, established over a period of time and acting in concert to commit terrorist offences. 'Structured group' shall mean a group that is not randomly formed for the immediate commission of an offence and that does not need to have formally defined roles for its members, continuity of its membership or a developed structure" (Council of the European Union 2002a).

As Chapter 1.1.1, on the brief historical outline of terrorism, has shown, the Al Qaeda network has been made responsible for the most devastating attacks in recent years. Al Qaeda is therefore the main representative of modern terrorism. It influences a number of smaller organizations, both directly, by supporting and steering their actions, and indirectly, by inspiring them with its ideology. For this reason, I will briefly present Al Qaeda – its structure and ideology – as this helps to understand today's terrorism in general as well as to understand the smaller, regional terrorist networks, which are often not even known before they commit the first attack.

1.2.1 Al Qaeda

The terror network Al Qaeda is usually said to be distinct in many ways from other terrorist organizations. This results mainly from the fact that the organization is a "moving target", which has adjusted its own structure and form several times (KURTH CRONIN 2006:7).

Al Qaeda is probably today's most famous terrorist movement, at least since it organized and committed the attacks on two World Trade Center towers and the Pentagon on September 11, 2001. Among experts it was also well known before, because Al Qaeda terrorists had already planned assaults for the millennium night in Los Angeles, Yemen and Jordan (HERMANN 2004:71). The sheer enormity of those plans and attacks shows that Al Qaeda must be a highly organized network with financial resources and highly motivated members, who are even willing to die. However, most knowledge about the movement is indefinite and a permanent matter of dispute.

It is, for example, not clear whether it is a cohesive network or a small movement, whether Osama bin Laden is Al Qaeda's most important leader and financier or just one among others. The scale of Al Qaeda's threat is also disputed: some argue that 9/11 was an exception, while others argue that it can become the rule (BYMAN 2003:140). Of course, this ignorance makes Al Qaeda an extremely dangerous enemy, who is difficult to fight, as no one knows whom exactly he fights against. Despite all this indeterminacy, some main information about the organization is known.

One of the network's founders is Osama bin Laden, a radical Islamic Saudi. In 1984, he had founded a guesthouse in Peshawar, Pakistan, at the border to Afghanistan, in order to support Arabs fighting against the Soviet Red Army in Afghanistan. In the following months, more and more guesthouses followed.

In 1988, Abdullah Azzam, a close comrade of Osama bin Laden, who was a cofounder of the guesthouses in Pakistan, called for the foundation of a "solid basis" in the journal "Al Jihad"[12]. Some academics see this text as the foundational text of

[12] The text *Al-qâ'ida al-sulba*, which translated means "The solid Basis" was published in the journal Al-Jihad, Number 41, 1988. For a long excerpt with detailed comments see KEPEL and MILELLI 2006: 259-267.

Al Qaeda. This view is disputed, as Azzam had used the expression Al Qaeda already earlier, with a different meaning (KEPEL and MILELLI 2006:264).

What is relatively well-known is that bin Laden went into exile in Sudan in the early 1990s and returned to Afghanistan in 1996, where he established military camps in order to educate and teach terrorist groups. Thenceforward he brought together different Islamists and terrorist groups and established a network of terrorists, with its base in Afghanistan[13] (SAGHI 2006:38). Thus, from about 1991 to 1996, Al Qaeda's main base was in Sudan and from 1996 to 2001, it was in Afghanistan (MERLOS 2006:69).

In 1998, Osama bin Laden enunciated a *fatwa*[14], a considered opinion, under the banner of "International Islamic Front for the Jihad against Jews and Crusaders", in which he called on all Muslims in the world to kill Americans and their allies (MUSHARBASH 2006:30). This *fatwa* shows that the network Al Qaeda predominantly fights against the US, which it associates with "crusaders". That explains the choice of symbolic targets such as the American warship USS Cole, the Pentagon or the World Trade Center, which exemplify the fight against American hegemony. In the same year of the *fatwa*, assaults on the American embassies in Nairobi, Kenya and Dar es Salaam, Tanzania, were committed by this network.

However, attacks on European targets, such as the bombing in Madrid, in March 2004 and London in July 2005, show that not only the US, but the Western world in general has become Al Qaeda's target[15]. Islamic states have also been chosen for attacks: Turkey and Indonesia have for example been victims of attacks. For Al Qaeda, these attacks are the goal in itself (BYMAN 2003:147).

In its beginning, Al Qaeda was organized hierarchically and it was led mainly from the base in Afghanistan, but after 9/11 the situation has changed, as a result of the Bush Administration's 'war on terror' (FALLOWS et al. 2005:9).

---

[13] The term "base", but also "rule" are actually two of the possible translations of the Arabic term al qâ'ida (Al Qaeda).

[14] It should be noted that Osama bin Laden is not entitled to proclaim a *fatwa*, as only specific Islamic scholars have the authority to do so. None of the signatories is such a scholar. See LAQUEUR 2004. Pp. 410-412 for the full statement by Shaykh Usamah Bin-Muhammad bin-Ladin, Ayman al-Zawahiri, Abu-Yasir Rifa'I Ahmad Taha, Shaykh Mir Hamzah and Fazlur Rahman.

[15] It has to be mentioned that is not clear whether the bombers of Madrid and London were merely inspired by Al Qaeda or whether Al Qaeda supported them in the organization of the attacks.

Especially the invasion of Afghanistan has forced the organization to adapt to the new circumstances and attacks during this Afghanistan War have proven that Al Qaeda was not destroyed in the war, but able to adjust to the new situation.

Today, it is a loose network, probably supported by several million radicals worldwide, with training camps in Pakistan and in Somalia (GUNARATNA 2002:8, 95; TAUS 2006:704).

In these camps, radical Islamists are instructed and some of them are recruited into higher ranks of the network. The members of these higher ranks organize the attacks. The number of those people is probably not more than a few hundred (HERMANN 2004:96). This core has relations to other radical Islamist groups all over the world, which in turn have relationships to regional and local groups. The exact size of supporters and direct or indirect members of Al Qaeda is therefore almost impossible to estimate. For the years 2004 and 2005 the International Institute for Strategic Studies has roughly estimated that Al Qaeda has 18000 trained terrorists and that the trend tends upwards (KEOHANE 2005:5), however there are also estimations that the number of trained terrorist is only 5000 to 10000 (NEUHOLD 2006:31). The system of Al Qaeda is thus similar to that of a hub and spokes, with Al Qaeda's core terrorist group as the hub and numerous regional and local radical Islamic groups, with similar, but not always identical aims, as the spokes. Due to this structure – a combination of hierarchy and global network – Al Qaeda can on the one hand easily replace terrorists at the higher ranks, that had been arrested or killed, and on the other hand, if one local or regional group breaks away, it is not of importance for the functioning of the whole network, because other parts of it are not affected at all. This makes it an extreme flexible network, which can act fast in many countries all over the world, because all the different local cells can act independently (HERMANN 2004:72).

The structure also shows that Osama bin Laden is probably less important than generally assumed and his death would by no means lead to the end of Al Qaeda. These are the main reasons why Al Qaeda is today the world's most dangerous terror group and why it is so difficult to fight against it (BYMAN 2003:153).

Regarding Al Qaeda and Europe, one can say that the organization itself is not present in Europe, in the sense that the core terrorists do not live and act here, but the ideology does exist in Europe (CLEMONS et al. 2005:47). Further, Al Qaeda recruits people from European countries. For example, one of the pilots of the 9/11 airplanes,

Mohammed Atta, lived in Hamburg, Germany. For the large scale terrorist attacks on public transportation systems in Europe, for example in Madrid and London, it is not clear whether they were committed by Al Qaeda or whether the terrorists had merely been inspired by Al Qaeda's ideology. Madrid's terrorists were members of a radical Islamic network and it is not known whether the network is directly linked to Al Qaeda (KAHL 2006:127). At least two of the four bombers of London had been in Pakistan before the attacks took place, and might have been trained in a camp there. In addition, after the attacks, Ayman al-Zawahiri, a leading Al Qaeda terrorist, supported the London suicide bombings (House of Commons 2005:20-21). It is striking that both these bombings have been committed by Islamic immigrants living in the respective cities (KEOHANE 2005:5).

As the EU is deeply involved in the fight against terrorism, by "using a whole array of tools, including diplomacy, the military, drying out financial sources, intelligence and aggressive law enforcement" (MÜLLER in Clemons et al. 2005:48), it most probably will also remain a target for further terrorist attacks. The thwarted terrorist acts in London in late June 2007 confirm this general impression.

1.2.2 Summary

Terrorist acts are usually committed by terrorist organizations. The term essentially means a structured group, which has been established over a period of time and acts in order to commit terrorist offences. The most dangerous terrorist group today is Al Qaeda.

Al Qaeda was founded during the 1980s in the border regions between Pakistan and Afghanistan and during the 1990s, Osama bin Laden, one of its founders, started to establish a network of different Islamic groups, with a base in Afghanistan. This network has permanently been expanded. After the events of 9/11 and the subsequent war in Afghanistan, the network had to adjust – it was no longer hierarchically organized, but transformed into a loose network. This structure, which is similar to a hub and spokes system, with Al Qaeda as the hub at the core and the numerous regional and local radical Islamic groups as the spokes, makes the network very robust and flexible: when one group breaks away the others are not affected.

The network has training camps, where recruits from all over the world are instructed. It is very difficult to estimate how many terrorists have been trained by Al Qaeda.

Europe has fallen victim to terrorist attacks, which have been ascribed to the broader network of Al Qaeda, and Al Qaeda's ideology exists in the EU. Immigrants residing in the EU or EU citizens might have been trained in one of the Al Qaeda camps.

The EU is in general deeply involved in the fight against terrorism and some of the EU reactions are directly targeted at Al Qaeda and those groups associated with Al Qaeda.

1.3 Terrorism as a Challenge to International Law

Whereas in the past the main threat to international peace was the states – wars took place mainly between states – this has changed considerably today: as the foregoing chapters have shown, today there is an increased threat from terrorist organizations. They are networked globally and they act on an international level, as a result it is nowadays impossible for single states alone to locate the responsible terrorists: international cooperation is needed. The framework for such cooperation in the fight against terrorism is international law. Since this is traditionally inter-state law, the change from states as actors, to non-state actors, poses a challenge to international law, as it has to adjust to the new circumstances. I will first briefly look at the classical inter-state regulations that are important in the fight against terrorism and then in a second step, in how far this body of law could already adapt to the new threat resulting from international criminal organizations.

1.3.1 The Prohibition of the Use of Force

In 1945, after the Second World War, the UN was founded, *inter alia* with the aim to prevent the world from further wars. For this reason, the Preamble of the UN Charter states that the UN wants to "save succeeding generations from the scourge of war, which twice in our lifetime has brought untold sorrow to mankind". Further, the first Article of the Charter, which summarizes the UN's purposes, underlines that they want to arrange for "international peace and security" (Article 1 (1) UNC).

Resulting from this general aim, the Charter regulates inter-state relations in a comprehensive way, and not only is war forbidden, but the use of force and even the threat of its use is forbidden:

> "All Members shall refrain in their international relations from the threat or use of force against the territorial integrity or political independence of any state, or in any other manner inconsistent with the purposes of the UN" (Article 2(4) UNC).

Meanwhile, this provision has become part of international customary law and is therefore not only binding for the UN member countries, but for all countries of the world (SHAW 2003:1018).

The prohibition of threat and use of force has even become a peremptory norm of international law and is part of *jus cogens*, as the International Court of Justice has confirmed in its judgment of the case concerning the military and paramilitary activities in and against Nicaragua (ICrtJ 1986).

The expression "force" in the Charter refers to military or armed force between different states. There is some controversy about the question whether force also implies economic force or other types of non-military force (SHAW 2003:1019).

The UN Charter allows for three exceptions to the general prohibition of the threat and use of force, one of which is self-defense.[16]

1.3.2 The Right of Self-Defense

The right of self-defense is regulated in Article 51 UNC, which states that

> "Nothing in the present Charter shall impair the inherent right of individual or collective self-defence if an armed attack occurs against a Member of the UN, until the Security Council has taken measures necessary to maintain international peace and security. Measures taken by Members in the exercise of this right of self-defence shall be immediately reported to the Security Council and shall not in any way affect the authority and responsibility of the Security Council under the present Charter to take at any time such action as it deems necessary in order to maintain or restore international peace and security."

[16] The other exceptions are according to Article 42 of the Charter collective measures authorized by the UNSC under Chapter VII of the Charter and according to Article 53, measures authorized by the SC under Chapter VIII for regional organizations. Article 53(2) and Article 107 also grant special rights to the victories of the Second World War with regard to use of force and the 'enemy states', but this provision has become obsolete. See STEIN and VON BUTTLAR (2005: 597).

Thus individual and collective self-defense is allowed in the aftermath of an armed attack. Whereas individual self-defense means that a state reacts to the attack without the help of other states, collective self-defense refers to the assistance of other states. This assistance can be granted either on an *ad hoc* basis or within organizations, such as the North-Atlantic Treaty Organization (STEIN and VON BUTTLAR 2005:298).

All actions of self-defense have to be limited in two respects. First, self-defense can only take place when an armed attack occurs, this means it must be at the present time. However, this does not mean that the action of self-defense has to take place immediately or on the same day, because a military strike has to be organized, especially when measures of collective self-defense are planned (i.e. WANDSCHER 2006:170). Second, self-defense has to be proportional to the foregoing armed attack.

The precondition for an act of self-defense is an armed attack. The expression 'armed attack' does not have any legal definition and it is not said in the Charter that it has to be committed by a state, but the fact that the Charter regulates inter-state relations has led to the general assumption that an armed attack is a coordinated and large-scale military action of one state against another (STEIN and VON BUTTLAR 2005:298; GAJA 2002).

Finally, there remains the problem of preventive self-defense and whether or under which circumstances it should be allowed. One distinguishes between anticipatory and preemptive self-defense. The former is self-defense against an attack that is deemed to be imminent, whereas the latter is against an attack that certainly will happen in the near future (DARBY 2005:30). According to the prerequisite given in the UN Charter, that self-defense can only be committed "if an armed attack occurs", both types of preventive self-defense seem to be prohibited.

Academics that are against all forms of preventive self-defense refer to this provision. In addition, they refer to Article 31(1) of the Vienna Convention on the Law of Treaties (1969), which says that a treaty must be ascertained "in the light of its object and purpose" and in the case of UN Charter, that is to prevent the unilateral use of force (BOTHE 2003:229).

However, if the armed attack is perceived as a "consistent pattern of violent terrorist action", then a state might act in anticipatory self-defense, because the single attacks that take place are subsumed under one ongoing attack and the time when nothing happens is just seen as a tactical break. In analogy with the regulations for inter-state wars, these breaks do not constitute the end of an armed attack and thus, the right of self-defense continues (STEIN and VON BUTTLAR 2005:328).

About measures of preventive self-defense in more general terms, there have been discussions long before the terrorist attacks of September 2001 were committed and most scholars have agreed that Article 51 UNC does not broadly allow for preventive self-defense, but that anticipatory self-defense might be necessary in some situations, whereas no right for preemptive self-defense exists (SCHACHTER 1984:1634; WANDSCHER 2006:175). Further, the UNSC has in some cases not condemned anticipatory self-defense[17].

On the other hand, the preemptive Israeli attack on a nuclear reactor under construction in Iraq in 1981 was "strongly condemned" by the UNSC as a violation of the UNC (United Nations 1981).

As a result of these two cases, one could see a limited authorization for anticipatory, but not for preemptive self-defense.[18]

Moreover, the state practice of several states speaks in favor of anticipatory self-defense, not only the US, but also France, Russia, Japan and others have reserved their rights for anticipatory self-defense in case of a serious threat (STEIN and VON BUTTLAR 2005:330).

The situation is different in case of preemptive self-defense. *De lege lata*, preemptive self-defense is not allowed (BOTHE 2003:232). Despite the fact that some states have supported the US in the preemptive war against Iraq in 2003, most states have disapproved this action and not agreed in stretching the *jus ad bellum* to Iraq (RATNER 2002:920). As a result, one can surely not claim that there is a rule of international customary law, allowing for such an act of preemptive self-defense (WANDSCHER 2006:312), as some American scholars do (DARBY 2005:33).

[17] One example for this is the Six-Day War in which Israel anticipatorily attacked Egypt, Syria and Jordan. In none of the SC Resolutions dealing with the Six-Day War can a condemnation for this act of preventive self-defense be found. The respective Resolutions of 1967 are 233, 234, 235, 236, 237 (United Nations 1967a, 1967b, 1967c, 1967d, 1967e).

[18] The supporters of this view often quote the Caroline Case in this context. In this case which took place in 1937, there had been laid down that there must be a "necessity of self-defense, instant, overwhelming, leaving no choice of means, and no moment for deliberation" (JENNINGS 1938: 89), in order to allow for measures of self-defense. This is one of the so-called Caroline criteria, which allows for anticipatory, but not for preemptive self defense and is part of international customary law. For more information see JENNINGS (1938).

Thus, the opinions in this question diverge. But in general, military actions should only be the *ultima ratio*, when criminal prosecution and international judicial cooperation cannot be applied or do not lead to useful results.

1.3.3 The Shift from State-Actors to International Criminal Organizations

In recent years, the number of inter-state wars has decreased, whereas the number of intra-state conflicts, civil wars and large-scale terrorist attacks has increased. As international law is essentially inter-state law, the increased threat of attacks from non-state actors poses a challenge to the interpretation of international law: terrorist organizations are "lacking formal or legal status as a state or as an agent of a state" (VON SCHORLEMER 2003:270).

In the past, when a state wanted to implement measures of self-defense resulting from terrorist attacks, the respective attack had to be attributed to a state.

This is regulated in the UN General Assembly Resolution 3314 (XXIX) of 1974. In Article 3 (g) of this Resolution, the General Assembly regulates that "(t)he sending by or on behalf of a State of armed bands, groups, irregulars or mercenaries, which carry out acts of armed force against another State of such gravity as to amount to the acts listed above[19], or its substantial involvement therein" allow the attacked state to take measures of self-defense against the state (United Nations 1974).

In the case between Nicaragua and the United States of America, the International Court of Justice affirmed that this regulation may be taken as international customary law (ICrtJ 1986: Article 195).

Thus, a mere basic involvement in the terrorist attack is not sufficient to allow for self-defense against the respective state (STEIN and VON BUTTLAR 2005:301). In August 2001, the International Law Commission has worked on draft articles about the "Responsibility of States for Internationally Wrongful Acts" (BEDERMAN 2002:817). According to this draft, a state can be held responsible

> "if the person or group of persons is in fact acting on the instructions of, or under the direction or control of, that State in carrying out the conduct"; "if the person or group of persons is in fact exercising elements of the governmental authority in the absence or default of the official authorities"; "if and to the extent that the State acknowledges and adopts the conduct in question as its own" (ILC 2002).

[19] The acts which qualify as an act of aggression are summarized in Article 3 a-f of the same resolution.

However, at the latest since the terrorist attacks on New York's World Trade Center in September 2001, it is a debated issue, whether such general criteria are sufficient. In case of the 9/11 attacks, the terrorists were neither sent by or on behalf of a state nor was the Afghan government substantially involved in the planning of the attacks. Further, from September to November 2001, Afghanistan did not have a government *de jure*. But, the *de facto* Taliban government did serve as a safe-haven for the presumable planners and actors of the attack, namely the Al Qaeda terrorists.

Moreover, the UNSC had demanded in 1998 already "that the Taliban stop providing sanctuary and training for international terrorists and their organizations" (United Nations 1998a), and has in later resolutions strongly condemned the support of terrorists by the Taliban Regime (United Nations 1999; 2000). The Taliban Regime did not comply with the resolutions and after the terrorist attacks, it even threatened the US by saying that similar attacks will follow. The Afghan government has thus ignored the decisions of the international community and publicly supported the terrorist acts. Even though this does not meet the General Assembly criteria to allow for self-defense, most states and academics agreed that in the light of these events, an act of self-defense could be allowed (TOMUSCHAT 2002:542)[20].

Two UNSC Resolutions that were adopted after the 9/11 attacks also confirm the right of self-defense in this case, namely Resolution 1368(2001) and 1373(2001) (United Nations 2001a, 2001b).

In these resolutions, the UNSC confirms the right to self-defense as a result of this specific terrorist attack, by referring to the "inherent right of individual or collective self-defense in accordance with the Charter". It has been doubted sometimes whether these Resolutions have legitimized an act of self-defense (e.g. CHARNEY 2001:836) because it is mentioned in the preambles rather than in the operative parts, but there was generally a consensus that the place of the provision does not play a role in this question (GRAY 2005:102). The terrorist attack thus has the status of an armed attack, even though it was not directly committed by a state. In none of the resolutions does the UNSC mention against whom the self-defense measures are allowed.

[20] It has sometimes also been claimed that the military response of the US can be justified with a "state of emergency" or "state of exception". However, the majority of academics, international institutions and states see self-defense as the proper justification for military reactions on terrorist acts, such as 9/11. See for example WANDSCHER (2006).

Resolution 1373 has further created obligations for all member states, which go beyond the existing conventions and it has established a committee of the UNSC, with a "broad and powerful mandate" (ROSAND 2003:341) to monitor the implementation. It requires all states to suppress the financing of international terrorist organizations. In order to comply with this resolution, the EU has established a list with names of groups and individuals, whose funds have to be frozen. The creation of such a list has evoked harsh criticism, because the procedure of setting up the list is not very transparent and there are a number of human rights problems involved in this procedure. Chapter 4.2, especially the sub-chapter 4.2.1, will deal with the different human rights concerns linked to this specific list.

Also the NATO (2001), which called on the member states that "the attack against the US was directed from abroad, it shall be regarded as an action covered by Article 5 of the Washington Treaty"[21], reacted on the assumption that the terrorist attack was an armed attack and allows for self-defense. Further, the EU has agreed that the US has a right of self-defense towards the Taliban (European Union 2001a).

In addition, the UNSC Resolution 1368(2001) "*stresses* that those responsible for aiding, supporting or harbouring the perpetrators, organizers and sponsors of these acts will be held accountable" (United Nations 2001a) and the Taliban actually "fit this designation" (FRANCK 2001:841) and Resolution 1373(2001) has similar provisions. All this argues for a loosening of the state accountability and that an adjustment to the new circumstances has taken place or is taking place (SCHOLZ 2006:36).

Accordingly, the invasion of Afghanistan as an act of self-defense, by the US and the NATO can be seen as legitimate act of collective self-defense. The fact that it started approximately one month after the 9/11 attacks is relatively unproblematic, as the US disclosed almost immediately after the assault that they will fight against the alleged criminals. Further, the action had to be planned. As a result, the invasion of Afghanistan was not an act of reprisal or retorsion. What should be noted is that the

[21] Article 5 of the Washington Treaty provides that: "The Parties agree that an armed attack against one or more of them in Europe or North America shall be considered an attack against them all and consequently they agree that, if such an armed attack occurs, each of them, in exercise of the right of individual or collective self-defence recognised by Article 51 of the Charter of the UN, will assist the Party or Parties so attacked by taking forthwith, individually and in concert with other Parties, such action as it deems necessary, including the use of armed force, to restore and maintain the security of the North Atlantic area" (NATO 1949).

state against the right of self-defense is exerted, does in turn not have a right of self-defense, against the state that acts in self-defense.

Of course, if the Taliban Regime had distanced itself from the attacks or even started to take actions against the terrorists on their territory, the situation would have been different. The same is true if the government had not known at all about the fact that terrorist organizations were acting on its territory (STEIN and VON BUTTLAR 2005:326).

There remains the question of self-defense in the case of terrorist acts taking place on territories free of sovereign rights or on a state's own territories. The prohibition of the use of force does not extend to these territories and measures of self-defense do not have to be justified by Article 51 UNC. Thus, internal conflicts with terrorist participation are not included in the regime of the general use of force; they are rather regulated by domestic law (SCHOLZ 2006:180-183).

1.3.4 Summary

The prohibition of the threat and use of force is today part of international customary law and even a peremptory norm of international law. Basically, two exceptions exist: states have a right to self-defense and the UNSC can authorize military action under certain circumstances.

In general, there are two limitations on self-defense: it has to take place immediately after an armed attack and it has to be proportionate. However, there are also two forms of preventive self-defense: anticipatory and preemptive self-defense. Despite the fact that the US and some other states claim that they have a right to preemptive self-defense, most academics agree that such a right does not exist and that the state practice of the US is not sufficient to change international customary law. Anticipatory self-defense is more accepted and it seems to be allowed in case that objective proof for an imminent attack exists.

International law is generally inter-state law and armed attacks of one state against another state can allow for self-defense. However, the increased threat of attacks from international terrorist organizations has initiated a change in this regard. Today, the majority of authors agree that all "acts of terrorism reaching the extent and gravity of the events on 11 September 2001 could be described as armed attack" (GUILLAUME 2004:546), which in turn allows for self-defense.

Thus, whereas in former times, terrorists had to be sent by or on behalf of a state to allow for self-defense against the respective state, this is today not longer a *conditio sine qua non*: if a state has enabled a terrorist group to plan and commit attacks by tolerating it on its territory, self-defense against the state is accepted, because it is partly responsible for the attacks (SIMMA 2003:105). The best example for this is the Afghanistan War, which started in 2001: "By failing to prevent the planning of terrorist activities on its territory and then failing either to try or to extradite the terrorists", Afghanistan has failed some of its fundamental international duties (MÉGRET 2002:22) and the US together with the NATO was allowed to invade the country as a measure of collective self-defense. However, self-defense should always be the *ultima ratio* and the principles of self-defense should be respected in all circumstances.

1.4 Summary

This chapter has aimed at giving the necessary background information to understand the fight against today's terrorism better.

In general, a terrorist act is a criminal act, leading to death or serious bodily harm of at least one person. It can also be a damage of public or private property. The action intimidates a certain population group or even the whole population of a country and aims at influencing the political and organizational decision-making. However, a clear definition on the international level could not be agreed upon so far, but on the EU level, a definition was adopted in 2002. This definition, laid down in the 'Framework Decision on combating terrorism', has been criticized widely, for being too vague and for violating human rights. This will be matter of examination in Chapter 4.1 of this paper.

The same Framework Decision provides a definition for terrorist organizations in Article 2, which is defined as "a structured group of more than two persons, established over a period of time and acting in concert to commit terrorist offences" (Council of the European Union 2002a). Today, the loose terrorist network of Al Qaeda is considered to be the most dangerous terrorist organization and it has been responsible for recent devastating attacks, the most important of which was 9/11.

For EU-wide or international cooperation and measures against terrorism, international law provides the framework. In this respect, the question of whether or under which circumstances a state is allowed to react with military action to a terrorist attack is of special importance. In general there is the *jus cogens* norm of prohibition of the use of force, enshrined in the UN Charter, but certain specified acts can allow for an exception of this prohibition. One such case is the right of self-defense. However, self-defense is only permitted in connection with the occurrence of an armed attack and armed attacks traditionally were only committed by states. For this reason, it is debated which conditions have to be fulfilled for a non-terrorist attack to qualify as armed attack. There is consensus that the 9/11 attacks do so and the US act of self-defense in the aftermath of 9/11 has been largely supported, for example by the UNSC in Resolution 1373(2001) and by the EU. This Resolution is of special interest for this thesis, as it specifies a number of obligations for all states and the EU has been criticized for violating human rights when implementing the respective Resolution. Chapter 4.2.1 will deal with the problems resulting from this specific Resolution in more detail.

2. EU Reactions to Terrorism

When the attacks on September 11, 2001 took place, the EU member states had already cooperated in the fight against terrorism for about 25 years. Despite the fact that the European Community was merely an economic community in the 1970s, member countries had already started cooperating as a result of the different terrorist groups acting at that time.

It was only with the implementation of the Maastricht Treaty, in 1993, that the EU has been given a legal basis to influence member states in their way of fighting terrorism (NILSSON 2006:73).

With the adoption of the Amsterdam Treaty in 1999, the competencies of the EU were even more expanded. However, as the EU is not a national state and as counter-terrorism lies at the very heart of internal security, the governments of the national states only slowly delegate more competencies to the supranational level. As a result, the EU itself has only very limited resources in terms of budget or personnel and therefore has to rely upon the member states for the implementation of EU measures (GREGORY 2005:106).

In the following sub-chapters, the main reactions and legislative measures of the EC and the EU respectively will be summarized. However, especially for the post 9/11 period, a comprehensive description of all measures is almost impossible as a multiplicity of different decisions, conventions and other instruments have been adopted in all three pillars in order to fight terrorism. I will therefore look at the key measures that have been decided, with a focus on those that might restrict fundamental rights. The focus will be on the time after the attacks on the US in September 2001; however, the aforementioned stages of cooperation have to be described as well, in order to show which efforts to fight terrorism had been made before 9/11 already. In addition, the Treaties of Maastricht and Amsterdam, which set up the legal framework of the EU, were adopted before 2001.

2.1 Cooperation in the Fight against Terrorism before 11 September 2001

In the early 1970s, terrorism started to be perceived as a common threat in the EC. Some of the most essential events in this regard are the attack on the Israeli participants of the Olympic Games in Munich, Germany in 1972, or the kidnapping of the employer representative Hanns-Martin Schleyer in Germany, combined with the hijacking of the German airplane *Landshut* in Palma de Mallorca in 1977. In addition, regional groups such as the ETA or the IRA started building networks among themselves and also with Palestinian terrorist organizations. As a result, the terrorist threat was not longer an internal one, within the boundaries of a certain country, but rather networked and acting across the boundaries of different states (MESSELKEN 2003:6).

Due to this increasing internationalization, the EC member states started cooperating on an inter-state basis in order to supplement what could not be achieved by the individual states alone (GAL-OR 1985:38).

In 1975, the Justice and Interior ministers of the member states decided to establish the so called TREVI[22] Group, the first meeting of which was held in June 1976 (BENYON et al. 1993:152). Thenceforward informal meetings took place twice a year at the ministerial level (KNELANGEN 2006:140).

Under the umbrella of these ministerial summits, different working groups were established, one of which was the Anti-Terrorism working group. The main aim of TREVI was to serve as a forum for the exchange of information and experiences. The group on terrorism also prepared a common European definition of the term, but it was never implemented (BENYON et al. 1993:154). In general, TREVI was a form of loose intergovernmental cooperation. It can, however, be seen as the "ancestor" of today's third pillar of the EU – the cooperation in Justice and Home Affairs, which was established with the Maastricht Treaty in 1992 (MONAR 2005a:388).

In 1979, the Police Working Group on Terrorism was established. It also held meetings twice a year and focused on the operational ways of countering terrorism. Its main aim was to "develop close links and trust between the specialist police forces

[22] According to some sources TREVI means "Terrorism, Radicalism, Extremism, Violence International", according to others, it is just an allusion to the famous fountain in Rome, because the group was established in Rome (BENYON et al. 1993:153).

in Europe involved in the prevention and investigation of terrorism" (BENYON et al.1993:188).

TREVI and the Police Working Group were practical working groups, without any legal force. The first legal means in Europe's fight against terrorism was adopted by the Council of Europe[23] in 1977: the 'European Convention on the Suppression of Terrorism', which mainly serves to facilitate extradition of terrorists and to foster cooperation in the fight against crime. However, Article 13 of the Convention regulates that the states have a right to refuse extradition. As a result, the application of the Convention is based on single-case decisions (MESSELKEN 2003:8) and indeed many countries have made use of this tool and have declared reservations (Council of Europe 2007b).

The topic of terrorism had taken a back seat during the 1980s, because of the decrease of the number of terrorist acts in most European states. As a result no necessity for a more intensified, regular cooperation in this area existed (KNELANGEN 2005:403). Furthermore, the introduction of the Schengen area in 1990 shifted the interest in the realm of police and judicial cooperation to the problems of the abolition of checks at common borders.

In 1992, the 'Treaty on European Union' was agreed. This treaty establishes the EU, based on a three pillar basis: the European Community, the Common Foreign and Security Policy and Justice and Home Affairs. The latter was changed with the 'Treaty of Amsterdam' in 1999 to 'Police and Judicial Cooperation in Criminal Matters'. With the entry into force of the Maastricht Treaty in 1993, cooperation with regard to terrorism was incorporated in the Union's institutional framework as a part of the third pillar.

The third pillar, Police and Judicial Cooperation, as well as the second pillar, the Common Foreign and Security Policy, are based on intergovernmental cooperation. In the first pillar, the EC, which basically refers to all economic related matters, the

[23] The Council of Europe is Europe's oldest political organization and it is not part of the European Union. Today it has 47 member states. All EU member states are Council of Europe member states and the Council of Europe has adopted a number of important Conventions, such as the European Convention on Human Rights. As all EU member states are Council of Europe members, the Conventions and decisions of the Council of Europe are relevant for the EU as well, even though the EU itself is not bound by them – the EU is for example so far not part of the European Convention on Human Rights – but the member states and thus indirectly the EU is also bound.

European member states have delegated their competencies to the EU. Thus, the first pillar is regulated supranational and the second and third only intergovernmental.

For decision-making and the implementation of decisions this merely intergovernmental cooperation means that contrary to the communitarized first pillar, the right of initiative is shared between the European Commission and the individual member states. When adopting a proposal, unanimity is required in the Council. The European Parliament only plays a marginal role. The Court of Justice of the European Communities only exercises powers in community law and is thus not involved in second and third pillar matters. The decisions that are made within this intergovernmental framework, are not immediately effective, rather they have to be converted into national law in a long and slow process of ratification (DEN BOER 2006:85). In the third pillar, the so-called 'Framework Decisions' are one instrument that has often been used in relation to terrorism, those decisions are binding for member states as to the outcome, but allow flexibility in how the outcome has to be achieved, which is different to the 'Action Plans', which are merely instruments of soft law (GREGORY 2005:108, 110).

In the provisions on the cooperation in justice and home affairs, terrorism is mentioned as common interest *expressis verbis* in the Maastricht Treaty (Article K.1 (9) TEU).

In more practical terms, these changes have led to an incorporation of the TREVI groups into the institutional framework, in the form of the Justice and Home Affairs Council of Ministers. This Council is at the top of a structure of different working groups (MONAR 2005a:392).

More important however was the creation of Europol, the European police office, which is a kind of international organization founded by the EU member states on the basis of intergovernmental cooperation, but out of the *acquis communautaire*. Its main task is the facilitation of cooperation between national police forces. It was only in 1999, that Europol could start working. In the same year, the tasks of Europol were extended to the fight against terrorism.

In the mid 1990s, two agreements on the extradition of criminals – and terrorists as a part of it – were decided. In 1995, the 'Convention on simplified Extradition Procedures between Member States' was adopted. It basically "obliges Member States to surrender persons sought for the purpose of extradition under simplified procedures provided for by the Convention on two conditions namely that the person in question consents to be extradited and that the requested State gives its agreement" (Council Act 1995).

In the following year, the 'Convention relating to extradition between the Member States of the EU' was adopted, which tries to abolish some of the reservations made by different countries under Article 13 of the 'European Convention on the Suppression of Terrorism' at least for EU member states. This Convention was replaced in January 2004 by the European Arrest Warrant, but in few cases it can still be applied (Council Act 1996). Contrary to the European Arrest Warrant, the 1995 and 1996 extradition treaties rest on the classical principle *aut dedere aut iudicare* – extradite or prosecute. Extradition was only made possible for offences qualifying as criminal in both countries – the requesting and the surrendering one.

An important step was the 'La Gomera Declaration', which was made after the Madrid European Council, in 1995. In this Declaration, combating terrorism is mentioned as one of the highest priorities of the EU and it calls for more intensive cooperation and information exchange (European Council 1995). This Declaration is basically the starting point for a judicial cooperation in the EU's fight against terrorism (ADAM 2005:31).

However, in general the European actions remained merely theoretical and the "La Gomera call for action remained essentially unanswered in the following years" (VENNEMANN 2004:227). It was the European Parliament that took the initiative in 1996 and requested the implementation of European and UN Conventions, as well as a general plan for countermeasures against terrorists, instead of *ad hoc* measures (MESSELKEN 2003:12). However, this did not lead to major changes.

In 1998, the "Action Plan of Vienna" was adopted in order to implement the provisions of the Amsterdam Treaty. It called for more capabilities and competencies for Europol and mentions terrorism as one of the priorities of Europol (European Commission and Council 1999). Following this Action Plan, the 'Presidency Conclusions of the Tampere European Council' in October 1999 were along the same lines with regard to terrorism by calling for more cooperation. Yet the Tampere European Council went a step further by deciding on the creation of Eurojust, which should be composed of national prosecutors, magistrates or police officers of the national authorities and serve as institutional basis for the facilitation of the coordination of national prosecuting authorities (European Council 1999). In 2001,

Pro-Eurojust, started the work on an interim-basis. Like Europol, Eurojust is located in The Hague.

In May 1999, the Treaty of Amsterdam, which was adopted in 1997, came into force. It revised the Maastricht Treaty and broadened the scope of combating terrorism. One of the objectives of the provisions of the Treaty is to provide "an area of freedom, security and justice" (Article K.1, Treaty of Amsterdam). Common action of the member states should be a means of reaching this aim and the fight against terrorism was mentioned as one of the tools in order to arrive at this "area of freedom, security and justice" (ibid).

Thus, the EU has been given the mandate to provide internal security within the third pillar (ADAM 2005:31). While this is a clear step forward in the scope of action of the EU, it conversely leads to a classical freedom / security dilemma, in the sense that in times of crisis, such as terrorist threats, the balance between freedom and security changes and tends to be re-established in favor of security. This is a well-known process in national states, but a new phenomenon for the EU (GREGORY 2005:109; KRIEGER 2004:52).

In the realm of the Common Foreign and Security Policy, the fight against terrorism is not explicitly mentioned, but in Article J1 (1) of the Amsterdam Treaty (1997) the strengthening of "the security of the Union in all ways" is mentioned as one objective and this can include action against security threats posed by terrorism.

More specifically, the Treaty of Amsterdam strengthens police and judicial cooperation and calls for the adoption "of measures establishing minimum rules relating to the constituent elements of criminal acts and to penalties in the field of organized crime, terrorism and illicit drug trafficking" (Article K.3(e) Treaty of Amsterdam).

The Treaty has further communitarized several measures and at least two of them, relating to the checks on persons at external borders and rules on visas, are of relevance in the fight against terrorism (Article 73j(2) Treaty of Amsterdam; MONAR 2005a:390).

In 2000, a Police Chiefs Task Force was established, which together with Europol should serve as a forum for experience exchange, planning common operations and so on. Further, the European Police College was established.

In June 2001, the Council of the EU (2001c) adopted the 'Framework Decision on money laundering, the identification, tracing, freezing, seizing and confiscation of instrumentalities and the proceeds of crime', in order to further suppress the financing of terrorism.

Despite the efforts of the EU, the implementation of adopted measures has so far been rather slow and cumbersome. As a result, the 'Committee on Citizens' Freedoms and Rights, Justice and Home Affairs' of the European Parliament (2001a) published a report on 5 July 2001 on the role of the EU in combating terrorism in which it regrets "the EU's slowness in responding to the terrorist threat and the fact that there is yet no coherent and legally binding set of coordinated measures" (Paragraph X, p. 11). The Committee called *inter alia* on the implementation of the decisions from Tampere. The European Parliament adopted the report on 5 September 2001.

2.2 Reactions after 9/11

11 September 2001 served as a "wake-up call" (ARCHICK 2003:3) and has led to a series of new legislative measures. The existence of a real "enemy" made the decision and enforcement of measures that were unpopular before possible among the different governments as well as towards the population (NILSSON 2005:449). The threat of these large-scale terrorist attacks required internal as well as external reaction from the EU and made "the formation of a genuine EU counterterrorism policy" (BURES 2006:60) possible. As a result, the decisions taken by the EU are characterized by a cross-pillarization. Many of the actions taken were not merely confined to terrorism, but in more general terms pertaining to the fight against organized crime.

The first EU reaction was a text, agreed one day after the attack by the General Affairs Council. In this declaration, the EU basically sympathizes with the US and offers them their help for finding the responsible persons for the attacks (European Union 2001a).

This position was reaffirmed by the 'EU joint declaration on the September 11 attacks in the US', on September 14, 2001, where it was assessed as an "assault on humanity" and the EU called on "all countries to redouble their efforts in the fight against terrorism" (European Union 2001b).

On September 20, 2001, an emergency Council meeting was convened and an extraordinary European Council the following day (NILSSON 2006:74). In the

‘Conclusions and Plan of Action’ of this latter meeting, the deep solidarity with the US is again expressed. The EU offers its help for a “riposte” against states “abetting, supporting and harbouring terrorists” (European Council 2001). The EU member states had different opinions about the legality of a military act of self-defense resulting from terrorist attacks, but they finally agreed on this formulation.[24] (KLEINE 2004:38).

Further, the ‘plan of action’ includes, in the realm of police and judicial cooperation, the adoption of a common definition of terrorism, the introduction of a European arrest warrant, cooperation and information exchange of European intelligence services, shared information between the member states and Europol, as well as a special terrorist team within Europol. In addition, international legal instruments, such as UN Conventions, should be finally implemented as soon as possible and necessary measures have to be taken to end the funding of terrorist networks, air security has to be strengthened and the fight against terrorism has to become part of the Common Foreign and Security Policy and the European Security and Defense Policy, because the “integration of all countries into a fair world system of security, prosperity and improved development is the condition for a strong and sustainable community for combating terrorism” (European Council 2001).

The ‘plan of action’ thus overlaps different areas of policy, but internal security is at the core. It has been updated several times and ultimately included more than 200 individual measures (MONAR 2005a:398).

On a meeting of the Justice and Home Affairs Council on December 6 and 7, 2001, the final setting-up of Eurojust was decided. On February 28, 2002 the decision was formally adopted. Further, by expanding the competencies, Eurojust has been granted a more active role. It can now call on national authorities to start investigations or to set up joint investigation teams, instead of merely serving as a facilitator of cooperation (ibid:402).

On 27 December 2001, the Council of the EU adopted a ‘Common Position on Combating Terrorism’. For the first time in history, the fight against terrorism is in this position categorized under the Common Foreign and Security Policy. This position mainly referred to the funding of terrorist organizations and the freezing of their assets (Council of the European Union 2001a). It is basically in line with the

---

[24] As the part on self-defense (Chapter 1.3) has shown, there is a broad consensus about this question today that such an act is legally justified.

UNSC Resolution 1373(2001)[25]. On the same day, a second common position regarding the measures to combat terrorism was published, also in order to implement the SC Resolution 1373(2001). The annex of this position contains a list of persons and groups that are classified as being terrorists (Council of the European Union 2001b). The position and the annex have been updated and revised several times. The list is disputed and it has been claimed that it is in breach with several fundamental rights. This common position, including the annex, was implemented by the EC Regulation 2580/2001 also on 27 December 2001. It is as controversial as the common position itself (European Community 2001).

In May 2002, EC Regulation 881(2002) established another list with terrorist names in order to freeze the funds of those individuals, entities and groups listed in the annex (European Community 2002). The list was set up by the UN and merely converted into EU law by the Council.[26] Human rights concerns have also been raised with regard to this list. All three lists will be discussed in more detail in Chapter 4.2.

The 'Council Framework Decision on Combating Terrorism' (Council of the European Union 2002a), which includes a definition of the term terrorism and was proposed in the plan of action on September 21, 2001, was only adopted in June 2002. It constitutes the cornerstone of the EU's fight against terrorism (DUMITRIU 2004:590). The adoption happened so late because for the European Parliament some of the provisions in the Decision went too far. In particular, the definition of terrorism was criticized as being too broad and in some passages the European Parliament (2001b) supported more protection of fundamental rights. A Council Statement was attached to the final text, in order to make sure that the right to demonstrate was not restricted by the decision. At a later point in this study, namely in Chapter 4.1, I will look at the definition and the amendment in more detail. Besides the comprehensive definition, the Framework Decision comprises an element of harmonization by giving guidelines for the minimal penalties for some terrorist offences.

Also in June 2002, the 'Framework Decision on the European Arrest Warrant and the Surrender Procedures between Member States' was adopted (Council of the

[25] See Chapter 1.3 for more information on SC Resolution 1373 (2001).

[26] The list was introduced by the UN with Resolution 1267(1999) and implemented in the EU in 2000 with the Council Regulation EC 337(2000) (United Nations 1999, European Community 2000). But whereas it referred only to the Taliban government and thus a state before, the updated version also refers to groups and individuals associated with Al Qaeda and Osama bin Laden.

European Union 2002b). The Arrest Warrant basically makes the arrest and transfer of suspects possible without the formal extradition procedures. This accelerates the whole extradition process. For a list of thirty-two different offences, extradition has to be executed even if the committed act constitutes a criminal act only in the requesting state – for these offences the principle of double criminality is thus abolished. In addition, nationals of the surrendering states can be extradited, which was not the case before and which is prohibited in the constitutions of some EU member states, for example Germany. The list includes terrorism. The Arrest Warrant has been criticized for not respecting fundamental rights in a sufficient way. For example the German Constitutional Court, the *Bundesverfassungsgericht* (2005), has judged after the implementation of the European Arrest Warrant in Germany that it does not guarantee fundamental rights anchored in Germany's basic law. The problems that the Arrest Warrant poses to fundamental rights will be a matter of evaluation in Chapter 4.3.

Furthermore, in June 2002 the 'Council Framework Decision on Joint Investigation teams', which was proposed in November 2001, was adopted (Council of the European Union 2002c). It stipulates that two or more member states can set up joint investigation teams for a limited time period. Combating terrorism is the priority of these teams (Preamble:§7).

The EU member states also agreed that a common European border guard would be necessary, in order to hinder illegal immigrants entering the EU territory (GRANT 2002:148). In October 2004, the 'European Agency for the Management of Operational Cooperation at the External Borders', FRONTEX, was finally adopted (European Community 2004a). FRONTEX has already become operational (NILSSON 2006:79).

On 15 May 2003, an Additional Protocol of the 1977 'European Convention on the Suppression of Terrorism' was adopted by the Council of Europe (2003a). This Protocol basically added to the existing Convention "all those crimes specified in the post-1977 anti-terrorist conventions concluded at UN-level" (TOMUSCHAT 2005:157).

The adoption of these different legal instruments shows that September 11, 2001 had a catalyzing effect on cooperation in the EU and in broader Europe.

None of the measures would have been taken with such a speed, without the attacks of 9/11 (NILSSON 2005:448). However, by the end of 2002, the two extradition

Conventions that were adopted in 1995 and 1996, had still not been ratified by all countries.

Besides these 'new' legislative measures, the existing EU structures started to be used more effectively to fight against international terrorism. The Council of the European Union (2002d) decided in December 2002 that national correspondents for Europol and Eurojust have to be designated and better provide the two authorities with information. In addition, the European Police College has included special antiterrorism trainings in its work programs.

The cooperation in intelligence services already started in November 2001 with meetings. In October 2003, it was agreed that the Council working parties on terrorism should produce a threat assessment report twice a year, the Police Chief Task Force should hold several meetings, and Europol should be better provided with data and information than before (MONAR 2005a:403-406).

External measures were also initiated, for example visits to Middle Eastern countries took place in the aftermath of the attacks, different meetings were held and declarations on bilateral and multilateral levels were adopted.

The "closest cooperation within the international system" (REES 2006:114) with regard to counterterrorism has been established between the EU and the US. The close cooperation that had been in existence before already was intensified. Only two months after the attacks, in November 2001, members of the provisional Eurojust agency went to Washington, for joint investigations. Since then, regular bilateral meetings have been held (MONAR 2005b:441).

The 2003 signed Agreements on Extradition and on Mutual Legal Assistance form the core of this cooperation. Such agreements on a bilateral basis, between the US and individual member states, had been in existence before, but a multilateral agreement between the EU and the US in such matters was new.

The negotiations on the 'Agreement on extradition between the European Union and the United States of America' (2003) proved especially difficult, because the European Convention on Human Rights does not allow for extradition to countries that have the death penalty. After having found some compromises however, the agreements could finally be signed. The 'Agreement on mutual legal assistance between the European Union and the United States of America' (2003) regulates different questions related to legal assistance, such as joint investigation teams, consultations and so forth.

Another controversial agreement had been negotiated by the European Commission concerning the transfer of personal data of passengers on transatlantic carriers. The Parliament of the EU adopted three critical resolutions relating to the agreement, expressing deep concerns about this problem[27]. The agreement on Passenger Name Records was finally signed in May 2004. In June 2004, the Parliament requested the Court of Justice of the European Communities to annul the agreement, because it violates fundamental data protection and procedural rights. The European Court of Justice (2006) has annulled the agreement.

The different EU-US agreements and their criticisms from a human rights point of view will be addressed in more detail in Chapter 4.4.

In sum, a number of new measures have been taken after 9/11, the most important of which were the 'Framework Decision on Combating Terrorism', the 'Framework Decision on the European Arrest Warrant and the Surrender Procedures between the Member States' and the 'Framework Decision of Joint Investigation Teams'. None of them was fully implemented when the attacks in March 2004 in Madrid happened. The instruments with regard to police and judicial cooperation that existed before 9/11 were also not sufficiently used (European Commission 2004a). This shows how slow the implementation process in the intergovernmental pillar of the EU is and that a few years after the 9/11 events, the member countries apparently did not see the necessity of implementing all legislative instruments in order to prevent terrorist attacks.

2.3 Reactions after the attacks in Madrid in March 2004 and London in July 2005

The attacks in March 2004 on commuter trains in Madrid and in London on busses and metros in July 2005, have boosted the pressure to better implement the existing anti-terrorism instruments and to decide on new ones (KAHL 2006:123).

On 11 March 2004, the terrorist attacks in Madrid took place. These bombings were the largest terrorist attacks in Spain ever: 191 people died and more than 1500 people were injured by attacks with 10 bombs in different trains (APARICIO 2004). With

[27] The 'resolution on transfer of personal data by airlines in the case of transatlantic flights' in March 2003, a 'state of negotiations' concerning the same agreement in October 2003 and a

this attack, for which Al Qaeda was made responsible, Al Qaeda had reached the EU. While these attacks were not completely unexpected, it laid open several deficiencies in the implementation of the European measures to prevent and fight terrorism. For example the 'Framework Decision on combating Terrorism' was only ratified by few countries, the same is true for the 'Framework Decision on Joint Investigation Teams' and many states did not provide Europol with the necessary information, to name just a few drawbacks.

On March 18, 2004 the European Commission decided on two memoranda. The first one called for the implementation of the so far adopted measures and suggested some new measures, basically the adoption of new Framework Decisions (European Commission 2004a). The second European Commission (2004b) memorandum is an action paper, consisting of five parts: a declaration of solidarity, again the call to make better use of the existing measures and of adopting new framework decisions, the strengthening of the fight against the financing of terrorist organizations, an improvement of coordination and cooperation in operative issues, and external action. On 25 March 2004, the Heads of States and Government formally adopted a 'Declaration on Combating Terrorism' during a European Council Meeting. The Declaration is in large parts an update of the existing action plan (European Council 2004). This roadmap contains 175 measures in order to fight terrorism (DEN BOER 2006:94). On 15 June 2004, a revised Action Plan on Combating Terrorism was adopted.

All these documents basically embrace the following elements: the highest degree of solidarity, the full implementation of the existing legislative acts and better provision of date to Europol and Eurojust. The Framework Decisions on attacks against information systems, on the confiscation of crime-related proceeds and on the mutual recognition of confiscation orders should be negotiated by June 2004. The negotiations for these different Framework Decisions had already started before the Madrid attacks, but no agreement could be reached.

In addition, a number of new legislative measures were proposed, including the retention of data by communication service providers, such as mobile phone companies, a European Criminal Record, in order to share the data about European convictions and facilitation of cross-border hot pursuit. Furthermore better protection

---

third resolution on the draft of the Commission decision in March 2004 (European Parliament 2003a, 2003b, 2004).

of witnesses in terrorist cases and the exchange of personal information, such as fingerprints and DNA, a system to exchange information on lost or stolen passports and the use of passenger data at border security were discussed issues (MONAR 2005b:445).

By the end of March, the European Commission had already proposed the first measures. One of the most important ones was the creation of a system of national bank account registries that allows for the identification of the real owner of the accounts and an information exchange between the member states and Europol and Eurojust (ibid).

These proposals – the registration of bank accounts, the European Criminal Record and the extension of sharing information and providing Europol and Eurojust with more information – were criticized by some national Parliaments and civil liberty groups for being not proportionate and somewhat incompatible with the European Convention on Human Rights[28]. However, these proposals have not been adopted so far and will therefore not be examined in more detail.

In order to make sure that the anti-terrorist measures will be fully implemented, the position of a counter-terrorism coordinator was introduced. The mandate was given to the Dutch Gijs de Vries. He has to report to the Council on a regular basis about the implementation of the Council decisions (ibid:446).

In November 2004, the Interior and Justice Minister of the EU decided on the so-called 'Hague Programme', which is a five-year plan covering different aspects of security and justice cooperation. It was finally adopted by the European Commission (2005) on 10 May 2005, together with an Action Plan setting out a timetable for the adoption and implementation of the main measures of the Hague Programme, which can be seen as further development of the Tampere Conclusions of 1999 (KNELANGEN 2005:408). It embraces ten different areas that should be of priority between 2005 and 2010. One of these priorities is the fight against terrorism. However, some of the other areas of action are also linked to terrorism, such as 'Internal Borders, External Borders and Visa' or 'Privacy and Security in Sharing Information'. The fight against terrorism in the Hague Programme essentially embraces five different 'Communications':

1. the prevention, preparedness and response to terrorist attacks,
2. the prevention and the fight against terrorist financing,

3. preparedness and consequence management,
4. critical infrastructure protection and
5. a pilot project for the victims of terrorist acts (European Commission 2005).

The strategy entails close cooperation with third countries in the fight against terrorism. The two main new principles in the Hague Programme, are the principle of solidarity, stressing the necessity of joint security and the principle of availability, which means that one member state can require another member state to transfer information. This principle of availability applies to six data categories: DNA, fingerprints, ballistics, vehicle registrations, telephone numbers and other communications data, and civil registers. According to the Hague Programme, by the end of 2007, this availability principle should work in the whole EU (ibid). The Criminal Record is one element of this principle, but this European Index System of criminal convictions has not been adopted so far.

In June 2007, the 'Prüm Treaty'[29] was incorporated in EU legislation – at least for the matters of DNA-profiles, fingerprints and vehicle number-plates. Until now, DNA profiles had to be shared via Interpol. The European Parliament has made a number of amendments, like a time limit for retention of data and inaccessibility of the database by third countries (European Parliament 2007b). In order to protect privacy a 'hit/no-hit' system will be introduced: this means if the police in country A works with a certain DNA sample, it can search the database and will receive information on whether another country holds information on this DNA sample – but not the name of the person. If a match is found, country A has to get in contact with the respective country and request further information. Only when specific requirements are fulfilled will countries be allowed to share information (ibid). However, the data systems of the EU countries are far from being compatible and it will take quite a while until implementation will be possible[30].

Finally, on the Council of Europe level, two Conventions were opened for signature on 16 May 2005: the 'Convention on the Prevention of Terrorism' and the

---

[28] See for example HOUSE OF COMMONS (2004) or HOUSE OF LORDS (2004).

[29] The Prüm Treaty was signed by Germany, Spain, France, Austria and the three Benelux states out of the EU framework on 27 May 2005.

[30] The human rights concerns that have been raised in relation to the incorporation of the Prüm Treaty will not be discussed in this book, because the adoption of the final text by the European Parliament took only place in June 2007.

'Convention on Laundering, Search, Seizure and Confiscation of the Proceeds from Crime and on the Financing of Terrorism' (Council of Europe 2005a, b).

Thus, when the terrorist bombings took place in London on 7 July 2005, which caused 56 casualties, including the four bombers and more than 700 injured people, the EU had already adopted a Comprehensive Action Plan for the next five years to combat terrorism (House of Commons 2005:2). Furthermore, the Council of Europe had also adopted new Conventions.

The EU's main aim in the aftermath of these attacks was therefore to speed up the ongoing work (NILSSON 2006:75).

Demands for loosening the existing human rights protection in order to fight terrorists more effectively also became louder. For example, the former British Home Secretary, CHARLES CLARKE (2005), called in the European Parliament on the revision of the 'European Convention on Human Rights' in the light of the terrorist threat, because "the right to be protected from torture and ill-treatment must be considered side by side with the right to be protected from the death and destruction caused by indiscriminate terrorism (..)".

Partly resulting from this, a 'Steering Committee on Human Rights' was called up in the Council of Europe. It was debated whether a new legal instrument should be established, allowing the deportation of suspects in countries that are known for applying torture, in case that these countries assure to not use torture for the deportee. In March 2006, the Committee rejected this proposal. Instead, it argued for the further ratification of human rights conventions (HEINZ 2007:14-15). In a statement in March 2006, the EU Commission underlined that the EU completely agrees with this view (ibid:15).

On 30 November 2005, the Council of the European Union (2005a) presented the new "EU counter-terrorism Strategy", which was adopted in December 2005. It reveals that the fight against terrorism is fourfold for the EU: prevent, protect, pursue and respond. These four dimensions are not limited to one pillar, but spread among the three pillars.

In the subtitle, the strategy explicitly refers to the protection of human rights: "The EU's strategic commitment: To combat terrorism globally while respecting human rights and making Europe safer, allowing its citizens to live in an area of freedom, security and justice." (Council of the European Union 2005a). A number of measures are mentioned in the four different categories, like *inter alia* inter-cultural dialogue and good governance in the prevention area or protection of external borders, by improved information exchange in the protection area. This includes passports with biometric data, a common Visa Information System and an updated Schengen Information System. In the persecution area, better use of existing authorities and implementation of adopted decisions are the most important means. Lastly, in order to effectively respond to terrorist acts, crisis coordination and the support and help for victims are the key priorities.

This strategy paper serves as a guideline adoption and implementation of measures in the future. It is a "mix of old and new ingredients" (DEN BOER 2006:99) and seems to lead to closer control and scrutiny of EU citizens and immigrants.

The different Information Systems are on their way to adoption. For example the text on the Visa Information System was adopted by the Parliament on 7 June 2007, a number of data protection issues have been included by the Parliament, especially because biometric data and fingerprints will be part of the database. The final agreement will probably be adopted very soon. In addition, a 'Framework Decision on Data Protection' is planned, in order to ensure data protection in all the different databases in all EU member countries (European Parliament 2007a). The Schengen Information System II will basically be an updated version of the already existing Schengen System. However, the technical development of this system will take some more time and only then will it be possible to finally adopt and implement it.

Data Protection, as well as an independent data protection body "are part and parcel of the Schengen Acquis" (European Commission 2007).

In November 2005, the "Exchange of information extracted from the criminal record" was adopted by the Council of the European Union (2005b). It basically improves the existing mechanisms on information exchange of convictions, but it does not equate with the database including the criminal records.

On 15 March 2006, the European Parliament and the Council of the EU have adopted a Directive on the retention of data (European Community 2006). It calls on a six-months-retention of telecommunication data, irrespective of whether someone is under suspicion or not. It has been claimed that this directive violates the right to privacy. This will be analyzed in detail in Chapter 4.5.

In order to further facilitate cooperation in criminal matters, the Proposal for a Council Framework Decision on the European Evidence Warrant was adopted in July 2006, which allows for obtaining documents and data for use in criminal proceedings

among the member states. This can basically lead to faster procedures (Council of the European Union 2006a).
In the light of terrorism and human rights, it must also be noted that in November 2005 it was made public that the US had secret detention facilities on the territory of two Council of Europe states, Romania and Poland (HUMAN RIGHTS WATCH 2005). Both countries were at that time not members of the EU, but they were accession countries and members of the European Convention on Human Rights. Furthermore, airplanes that have allegedly been used by the CIA to transport prisoners landed in different EU member states, among them Germany, Spain and the United Kingdom.
The reaction of the EU to this practice of the US was very comprehensive. Different legal opinions and reports were elaborated. The main findings were that between September 2001 and April 2006 more than 1000 unannounced flights by the CIA over European territory had taken place and that presumably fourteen Council of Europe member states were involved. It seems to have been proven that human rights were violated. The European Parliament explicitly criticized some countries – among them Germany, Spain and Sweden for not having controlled the flights as should have been done (HEINZ 2007:28).

2.4 Summary

European cooperation in the fight against terrorism had already started in the 1970s, in the form of loose intergovernmental cooperation – outside of the by then existing community framework. It was only in 1993, with the creation of the EU that this cooperation was incorporated in the legal framework. The Amsterdam Treaty, which came into effect in 1999, broadened the legal basis of the EU in the third pillar, the Police and Judicial Cooperation in Criminal Matters. A number of measures related to the fight against terrorism were adopted at this time, most notably the establishment of Europol and Eurojust and the adoption of extradition agreements, facilitating the by then existing extradition practice.
When the 9/11 attacks took place, the EU already had experience in anti-terrorism cooperation, but due to the new quality of the attacks, for the first time in history, the EU had to enact measures spread over all three pillars in the fight against terrorism (KNELANGEN 2005:405).

All decisions and instruments with regard to terrorism before and after 9/11, show that the EU considers terrorism as a specific type of crime, which has to be prosecuted by the police and legal authorities. The EU does not rule out a war in the fight against terrorism – it did support the US in their riposte against Afghanistan – but primarily criminal proceedings are applied.

One of the first post-9/11 reactions was support for an American act of self-defense. Further, Eurojust was finally set up and the information and data exchange was to be enhanced. A more comprehensive action plan was also agreed. Some measures of this plan are questionable from a human rights point of view and will need further evaluation.

First, in December 2001 the EU set up a list with names of individuals and groups that are classified as being terrorists and whose funds have to be frozen. In 2002, a similar list – limited to individuals, groups and entities associated with Al Qaeda, Osama bin Laden or the Taliban – that was set up by the UN, was implemented on the EU level.

Second, the EU laid down a definition of terrorism, which has been criticized for being too broad and for violating the European Convention of Human Rights.

Third, the agreement on a European Arrest Warrant, which abolished the principle of double criminality for certain offences, was reached. It has been criticized for violating fundamental rights and, for example, in Germany the Constitutional Court has annulled the implementation of this Arrest Warrant.

Also resulting from the 9/11 attacks, the EU has increased cooperation with the US, basically by adopting different agreements. Especially the 'Agreement on Passenger Name Records' was harshly criticized and even annulled by the Court of Justice, but the two other agreements, on mutual legal assistance and on extradition can be criticized from a human rights perspective, were also criticized because of the existence of the death penalty in the US and because of lower data protection standards.

The actions that were taken in the aftermath of the Madrid and London attacks have mostly been calling on the implementation of existing decisions and conventions. In addition, the existing institutions, like Europol and Eurojust have not been used exhaustively. The new measures that have been taken in this time period, most notably relate to sharing of information and data. A number of the proposed measures have not been finally adopted so far. One measure that has been adopted and criticized for being in breach with the European Convention on Human Rights is the directive on data retention. This will be the fifth measure, analyzed in Chapter 4.

The CIA flights will not be a part of the evaluation as individual member states are affected, but the EU is not directly affected. However it should be positively acknowledged that the EU has examined and tried to lay open the incidents.

3. The Law of Human Rights and Fundamental Freedoms

As the aim of this book is to analyze the European reactions on terrorism after 9/11 in the light of human rights law, international and European law of human rights and fundamental freedoms has to be introduced, in order to provide a basis for the assessment of the EU reactions that is going to follow in Chapter 4.

Human rights law is a part of international law. It basically refers to "agreed values, standards or rules regulating the conduct of states" (BAEHR 1999:1) towards all individuals. It restricts the freedom of states and their room for action by giving them a framework of rights that have to be guaranteed, and on the other hand prohibiting the states certain conducts.

Human right law exists – like international law in general – in form of treaty law, customary law and soft law, such as UN General Assembly Resolutions (POKEMPNER 2002:19). Some obligations under human rights law, such as the prohibition of genocide and the prohibition of slavery, are part of *jus cogens* as well as the right to life and freedom from *ex post facto* laws. The prohibition of torture and inhuman treatment and of extreme racial discrimination, are also considered as peremptory norms of international law (STEIN and VON BUTTLAR 2005:389).

In peacetime, human rights law has to be applied in its full scope. A derogation of rights is only allowed in case of a declared national emergency[31] and not all rights are derogable. In wartime, international human rights law coexists with international humanitarian law. But as *durante bello* usually a state of emergency is declared, only the non-derogable human rights have to be guaranteed and they are supplemented by the guarantees that International Humanitarian Law makes. Humanitarian Law thus serves as a *lex specialis*, which is only applicable under the condition that an armed conflict takes place (POKEMPNER 2002:19). International Humanitarian Law is essentially regulated by the Geneva Conventions and its Additional Protocols.

As the EU has not declared a state of emergency, it has to guarantee and fulfill the full scope of its human rights obligations. The EU member countries are bound by several treaties guaranteeing fundamental rights to its citizens; these are on the one hand international agreements and on the other hand regional ones, but on both levels

[31] The circumstances under which a state of national emergency can be proclaimed are usually specified in domestic law. In most general terms, in time of war or after extreme natural

the treaties generally contain very similar obligations. I will therefore only briefly look at international obligations in the following part and then describe the European human rights law in more detail. However, this chapter serves mainly as an overview and will not explain every single right comprehensively.

It should be additionally noted that many of the younger agreements dealing with terrorism do not fail in stressing the importance of the protection of human rights in the fight against terrorism (BOURLOYANNIS-VRAILAS 2004:17). This is the case for the UN, as well as on the regional level. In the beginning it was "limited to the guarantee of fair treatment"[32] (SEIBERT-FOHR 2004:127). Later, the reference to human rights was extended and in the more recent agreements, reference is made to the international human rights standards, for example in the 'International Convention for the Suppression of Terrorist Bombing'[33] (United Nations 1998b) or on the EU level, in the 2002 'Framework Decision on Combating Terrorism'[34] (Council of the European Union 2002a). These provisions show that the fight against terrorism does not necessarily lead to an abrogation from human rights law.

3.1 International Human Rights Law

Different International Declarations and Covenants on human rights exist. First of all, the UN Charter refers to the protection of human rights in different articles. For example Article 1 UNC mentions the promotion and encouragement of respect for human rights and fundamental freedoms as one of the purposes of the UN.

The cornerstone of global human rights protection is the 'Universal Declaration of Human Rights', which was adopted in 1948 by the General Assembly (United Nations 1948). From a legal point of view, it was merely a recommendation, rather than a binding legal instrument. But today, this declaration is binding, either as a part of customary law or as a general principle of international law (SHAW 2003:260).

The main intention of the UDHR was to serve as "a common standard of achievement for all peoples and all nations" (United Nations 1948).

disasters, the state of emergency is proclaimed. In such cases the UN Secretary General has to be informed. An emergency situation is usually for a limited period of time.

[32] For example in the Convention on the Prevention and Punishment of Crimes against International Protected Persons (1973).

[33] Article 14.

[34] Preamble and Article 1(2).

It consists of thirty articles and covers a whole range of different rights. Starting with "traditional rights and freedoms" (TOMUSCHAT 2003a:29) such as liberty and security (Article 3), prohibition of torture (Article 5) or asylum (Article 14). Article 21 then refers to the right of political participation and the following articles cover social and economic rights, such as the right to equal pay (Article 23) or the right to education (Article 26).

Since the UDHR was not adopted as a binding, legal instrument, the UN aimed at incorporating its provisions in legally binding international treaties. As a result, in 1966 the General Assembly adopted two Covenants on human rights: the 'International Covenant on Civil and Political Rights' and the 'International Covenant on Economic, Social and Cultural Rights' (United Nations 1966a, b).

In large parts, these two treaties include the provisions of the UDHR, but they also add some rights, like the right to self-determination, and do not mention others that are part of the UDHR, such as the right to seek asylum.

The 'International Covenant on Civil and Political Rights' includes rights like the right to self-determination, the right to life, the prohibition of torture and slavery, the right to liberty and security of the person, due process, freedom of thought, of conscience, of religion, of association and the protection of minorities.

The 'International Covenant on Economic, Social and Cultural Rights' basically covers the rights to self-determination, to work, to social security, to an adequate standard of living, to education, to take part in cultural life and to enjoy the benefits of scientific progress.

The two treaties entered into force in 1976. The 'Covenant on Civil and Political Rights' is today ratified by 160 countries, and the 'Covenant on Economic, Social and Cultural Rights' has 156 parties (OHCHR 2007a, b). The additional Protocols have been ratified by fewer countries.

Apart from these general conventions, more specific ones have been adopted, like the 'Convention on the Prevention and Punishment of the Crime of Genocide', the 'International Convention on the Elimination of all forms of Racial Discrimination' or the 'Convention against Torture and other Cruel, Inhuman or Degrading Treatment or Punishment', among others.

In addition, different political bodies and expert bodies have been established under the auspices of the UN in order to observe the human rights situation and to promote human rights.

3.2 European Human Rights Law

In Europe, different regional conventions regulate human rights law. Most of them are Council of Europe agreements and thus not only EU member states, but all Council of Europe countries have ratified them. From both, the aspect of protected rights and the aspect of implementation, Europe has the world's most effective human rights protection system (STEIN and VON BUTTLAR 2005:400).

In the following sub-chapters I will first look at human rights law in Europe in general, with special focus on the EU, by taking into consideration European case-law. Then I will present the Council of Europe 'Convention for the Protection of Human Rights and Fundamental Freedoms' and the 'Charter of Fundamental Rights of the European Union'.

3.2.1 Council of Europe and EU Human Rights Law

When the European Economic Community was established in 1957, the 'European Convention on Human Rights' had already entered into force. The EC itself however did not become member of it. The European Court of Justice has nevertheless made clear in some of its judgments that respect for human rights is an integral part of the law that is protected by the Court and thus an integral part of the Community. For example in the case *Internationale Handelsgesellschaft* the Court stated that:

> "In fact, respect for fundamental rights forms an integral part of the general principles of law protected by the Court of Justice. The protection of such rights, whilst inspired by the constitutional traditions common to Member States, must be insured within the framework of the structure and objectives of the Community" (European Court of Justice 1970).

In 1974, the European Court of Justice found that in addition to the constitutional traditions common to the member states, "international treaties for the protection of human rights on which the Member States have collaborated or of which they are signatories, can supply guidelines which should be followed within the framework of Community law."

The 'Convention for the Protection of Human Rights and Fundamental Freedoms', or 'European Convention on Human Rights' as it also called, can clearly be seen as one of the most important treaties in this respect and the Court of Justice has in later judgments referred to this specific convention[35]. It has also been taken into consideration that the EU itself should become a member of the 'European Convention on Human Rights', for example the former President of the European Court of Human Rights, Luzius Wildhaber, has called on the accession of the EU to ensure a coherent protection of human rights (ECrtHR 2003a). Even though the EU is not signatory of this Convention, it is somehow bound by it because the Convention is explicitly mentioned in the Maastricht Treaty, under Title I, Article 6, which states that

> "1. The Union is founded on the principles of liberty, democracy, respect for human rights and fundamental freedoms, and the rule of law, principles which are common to the Member States.
>
> 2. The Union shall respect fundamental rights, as guaranteed by the European Convention for the Protection of Human Rights and Fundamental Freedoms signed in Rome on 4 November 1950 and as they result from the constitutional traditions common to the member states, as general principles of Community law."

The 'European Convention on Human Rights' constitutes the earliest and main regional human rights instrument in post-Second World War Europe. It was signed on 4 November 1950 and entered into force in September 1953. This is the most important agreement from a human rights point of view in Europe. It has been amended several times with different Protocols and predominantly covers civil and political rights.

Social and economic rights were almost not covered in the 'European Convention of Human Rights' and in the late 1950s, the European countries realized that they should not "treat economic and social rights light-handedly as rights of lesser importance" (TOMUSCHAT 2003a:30). As a result, the 'European Social Charter' was developed, which was signed on 8 October 1961 as the second cornerstone of European human rights law. Due to the economic differences between Council of Europe members, the negotiations of this Charter were cumbersome and the individual states are not obliged to implement all of the articles of the Charter. This

[35] For example in Regina v Kent Kirk (1984) or X v Commission (1994) (ECJ 1984, 1992).

makes the Charter a relatively difficult accessible instrument, because different states have ratified different Articles.[36].

In addition to these two main Conventions, covering a multitude of fundamental rights, two more specific conventions have been established: the 'European Convention for the Prevention of Torture and Inhuman and Degrading Treatment or Punishment', which came into force in 1989 and the 'Council of Europe Framework Convention for the Protection of National Minorities', which became effective in February 1998.

The European Union specifically has adopted the 'Charter of Fundamental Rights' in December 2000, which has so far not been legally binding. However, on the last European Council, in June 2007, it was decided to make the Charter a legally binding instrument. Great Britain will however be excluded from this binding character.

The latest human rights framework has been negotiated and adopted in 2002 by the Council of Europe (2002a). These-so called 'Council of Europe guidelines on Human Rights and the Fight against Terrorism' are non-binding, but serve as a framework for the European states and their anti-terrorism policies. They are essentially a "compilation drawing upon existing treaty law, case law, principles and practice" (EATON 2004:29). They are thus not new and as they are based on existing binding texts, they merely serve as a "clear and accessible" (ibid) summary. For this reason, the guidelines will not be explained in detail within the following sub-chapters.

[36] The European Social Charter only covers social and economic rights. These rights are – so far – not endangered by the EU in the fight against terrorism. It lists nineteen rights and the contracting parties have to consider themselves bound by at least five key articles out of seven specific articles and in general only ten out of the first nineteen articles. Most generally, the Social Charter covers labor and trade union rights, the protection of children and young persons, of employed women, of disabled persons, of mothers and the family and of migrant workers and their families. Social security rights, in terms of the right to social and medical assistance and the right to benefit from social welfare services are also included (Council of Europe 1961). Additional Protocols were adopted and a revised Charter was adopted and has been ratified by 27 countries so far (Council of Europe 2007a).

3.2.2 Convention for the Protection of Human Rights and Fundamental Freedoms

The 'European Convention on Human Rights' is the most important treaty with regard to human rights in Europe. It builds the basis for a European public order (STEIN and VON BUTTLAR 2005:401).

The rights covered in the Convention on Human Rights are the right to life (Article 2), the prohibition of torture (Article 3), prohibition of slavery and forced labor (Article 4), right to liberty and security (Article 5), the right to a fair trial (Article 6), no punishment without law (Article 7), right to respect for private and family life (Article 8), the freedom of thought, conscience and religion (Article 9), freedom of expression (Article 10), freedom of association and assembly (Article 11), the right to marry (Article 12), right to an effective remedy (Article 13) and prohibition of discrimination (Article 14).

Article 15 is concerned with the derogation of human rights in times of emergency. In essence, the right to life, the prohibition of torture and slavery and the principle of no punishment without law, can under no circumstances be derogated.

Furthermore, the Convention regulates the establishment and work of the European Court of Human Rights (Articles 19-51) (Council of Europe 2003b).

This Convention of 1950 has been amended by several protocols. The first Protocol was signed in 1952 and covers the protection of property, the right to education and the right to free elections. Protocol Number 4 was agreed upon in 1963. It prohibits imprisonment for debt, the expulsion of nationals and the collective expulsion of Aliens and guarantees the freedom of movement. The next amendment was made with Protocol Number 6 in 1983. With this Protocol, the death penalty has been abolished in peacetimes. No derogation of this provision is allowed in states of emergency. In 1984, Protocol 7 has included different procedural rights. It guarantees some procedural safeguards for aliens that are to be expelled from a European country, the right to appeal in criminal matters, compensation in case of wrongful conviction, the right to not be tried or punished twice and the equality between spouses.

In 2000, the general prohibition of discrimination has become a guaranteed human right with the Protocol Number 12. In 2002, Protocol Number 13 completely abolished the death penalty. Also in wartime, exceptions are not longer allowed.

While the Convention and the Additional Protocols are binding, once they have been ratified, the European Court of Human Rights has always emphasized that it is a living instrument, that "has to be interpreted in the light of present-day conditions" (SHAW 2003:323). However, not all Council of Europe member countries, even not all EU member countries, have ratified all the Additional Protocols (Council of Europe 2006).

The European Court of Human Rights, which has been established with the European Convention on Human Rights, is an international court, based in Strasbourg. Each Council of Europe state sends one judge to the Court, but the judges do not represent the respective state, rather they act independently of their states. The Court was set up in order to safeguard the application of the European Convention on Human Rights. Individuals, legal entities, as well as states can lodge applications when they have fallen victim to a human rights violation committed by a state that is bound by the Convention. Before lodging an application at the Court of Human Rights, all domestic remedies in the accused state must have been exhausted. The number of applications has been growing since the establishment of the court. In 2006, 50500 applications had been lodged, that is 11% more than in 2005 (ECrtHR 2006). The Court and its judgments thus play a significant role.

3.2.3 The Charter of Fundamental Rights of the European Union

The 'Charter of Fundamental Rights' was adopted on 7 December 2000 at a European Council meeting in Nice. It consists of seven chapters: Dignity, Freedom, Equality, Solidarity, Citizen's Rights, Justice and General Provisions (European Union 2000).

The different chapters cover the human rights and fundamental freedoms that are also protected under the European Convention of Human Rights, but the Charter goes further.

Human dignity includes the right to life, the right to the integrity of the person, the prohibitions of torture and inhuman treatment and of slavery (Articles 1-5). The chapter on Freedoms covers the right to liberty and security, the respect for private and family life, data protection, the right to marry, the freedom of thought, conscience and religion, the freedom of expression and information, the freedom of assembly and association, freedom of arts and sciences, the right to education, the freedom to choose an occupation, to engage in work and to conduct a business, the right to property, the right to asylum, protection in case of expulsions, removal or extradition (Articles 6-19).

The Equality Chapter guarantees non-discrimination and equality before the law and of men and women. It covers the respect of cultural, linguistic and religious diversity, the rights of the child and of the elderly and the integration of disabled people (Articles 20-26).

The Chapter on Solidarity refers to different workers rights, like the protection of young people, the prohibition of child work and fair and just working conditions. It further ensures social assistance, access to health care, and protection of consumers as well as the environment (Articles 27-38).

The fifth chapter regulates the citizen's rights. This includes political rights, such as the right to vote or to serve as a candidate, right to good administration, the right of the access to documents, the freedom of movement and it ensures diplomatic protection (Articles 39-46).

Chapter six mainly covers procedural rights, such as the right to a fair trial or the presumption of innocence. It guarantees the principle of proportionality and legality of criminal offences and penalties, and the right to be not punished twice for the same offence (Articles 47-50).

Finally, the last chapter provides the general provisions about the application and restrictions of the fundamental rights.

So far, this 'Charter of Fundamental Rights' has not been legally binding – neither for the member states nor for the supranational EU organs, because such a Charter has not been envisaged in the treaties on European integration and the institutions of the EU do not have the competence to amend those treaties (TOMUSCHAT 2003b:319). The EU organs should, in a voluntary form, stick to the Charter and the European Court of Justice and the European Court of First Instance should consult the Charter for interpretation in their decisions and judgments (STEIN and VON BUTTLAR 2005:417). However, on the European Council in June 2007, it was decided to make the Charter a legally binding instrument within the EU – except for Great Britain. The Charter can therefore serve as a point of reference when evaluating the EU reactions to terrorism.

3.3 Summary

Human rights law is a part of international law. Some provisions of human rights law are today part of *jus cogens*: the prohibition of genocide, of slavery, of torture and of extreme racial discrimination, as well as freedom from *ex post facto* laws. States are obliged to secure human rights standards that are defined in the different agreements – this implies that states are obliged to combat terrorism, because terrorist attacks are a threat to human rights, for example the right to life. States protect fundamental rights by prosecuting terrorists and at the same time, they are bound by those fundamental rights and have to comply with them (SEIBERT-FOHR 2004:136).

On a global level, the Universal Declaration of Human Rights gives a broad framework of human rights. Even though it was not legally binding when it was adopted, it has today become part of customary law and its provisions have been integrated in binding treaties. The two most important treaties in this respect are the 'International Covenant on Civil and Political Rights' and the 'International Covenant of Economic, Social and Cultural Rights'.

In Europe, a regional system of human rights protection has evolved. The 'European Convention on Human Rights' forms the cornerstone in this respect. This agreement focuses mainly on political and civil rights and has therefore been followed by the' European Social Charter'. The youngest agreement by the Council of Europe is the 'Human Rights and the Fight against Terrorism Guidelines', which basically summarize existing human rights law. On the EU level, the 'Charter of Fundamental Rights of the European Union' was adopted in 2000.

The different treaties cover a multitude of fundamental rights – civil, political, economic, social and cultural ones.

The EU itself is not a member of the different human rights treaties, but as almost all member states have ratified almost all of the international and European treaties, the EU is bound by them. Further, the Maastricht Treaty calls on the EU to respect the European Convention of Human Rights and European case-law has emphasized that.

The EU Charter of Fundamental Freedoms is not currently legally binding, but it can be used by the Courts and it lists rights that in many European member states are part of the constitutional law. For this reason, it can serve, as additional framework for the evaluation of European policy in the following chapter. Furthermore, it is going to be binding in the near future.

4. European Reactions in the Light of European Human Rights Law

As suggested in the foregoing chapters, some of the European reactions to terrorism have been criticized for not respecting human rights in a sufficient way. The main critics came from the European Parliament, but national Parliaments and non-governmental organizations, such as Statewatch or independent expert networks, also made critisisms. Academics have also raised concerns with regard to specific EU measures.

Since there is no state of emergency in the EU, and so far in the fight against global terrorism there has not been any reason to proclaim one in the EU, the EU has to fulfill the full obligations under human rights law and no derogations are allowed. However, not all human rights are absolute and some of them can be restricted under certain circumstances – the fight against terrorism might qualify for this.

Different declarations stress the necessity of respecting human rights, like the so-called 'Berlin Declaration' on upholding human rights and the rule of law in combating terrorism (ICJ 2005), the above mentioned 'Council of Europe Guidelines on human rights in the fight against terrorism', or on the UN level, the annex of the SC Resolution 1456 which states in Paragraph 6 that

> "States must ensure that any measure taken to combat terrorism comply with all their obligations under international law, and should adopt such measures in accordance with international law, in particular international human rights, refugee and humanitarian law" (United Nations 2003).

Thus, severe restrictions on fundamental rights are by no means acceptable in Europe's current situation.

It should be recapitulated in the beginning of this evaluation, that in the third pillar, the Parliament only plays a marginal role and that the European Court of Justice is not competent, because third pillar matters are not part of the communitarized area. The democratic control and accountability over EU actions therefore lag behind the competencies that the EU has in this area (NÍ AOLÁIN 2003:74) and the institutional balance is "still very inadequate" (CFR-CDF 2003:9).

In the following sub-chapters I will shed some light on the relation between human rights norms and those measures that have been criticized for violating human rights

and evaluate whether those measures are in breach of international human rights law and / or European human rights law, as a part of international law.
The measures taken by the EU, which will be evaluated in the following paragraphs are the common definition of terrorism, the lists of terrorists and terrorist organizations, this includes the lists established by the EU, as well as the list that the UN has set up and that the EU has implemented, the European Arrest Warrant, the EU-US agreements concerning extradition, mutual legal assistance and the Passenger Name Records and finally data protection issues, especially the retention of data.

4.1 The Framework Decision on Combating Terrorism

The 'Framework Decision on Combating Terrorism' was adopted on 13 June 2002 in Luxembourg. It consists of a Preamble and eleven Articles. Article 1 lays down a definition of terrorism and Article 2 of terrorist groups. Article 3 refers to offences linked to terrorist activities and Article 4 makes also inciting, aiding or abetting and attempting to commit one of the offences, defined in Articles 1-3 punishable. The remaining articles basically regulate how such terrorist offences should be punished in the member states and include general provisions on implementation and entry into force (Council of the European Union 2002a). Article 1 constitutes the core of the Decision, as it defines "terrorist offences" and the offences mentioned in Article 2-4 necessarily need to be connected to a terrorist offence as defined in Article 1.[37]
Actions of armed forces during armed conflict are excluded from being considered as terrorist offences.
The Framework Decision thus leads to a minimum harmonization in criminal matters related to terrorist offences. Such a minimum harmonization in the third pillar is provided for under Title VI of the Treaty of Amsterdam.

4.1.1 The Definition of Terrorism

The text of the Framework Decision was proposed by the European Commission in September 2001, then "speedily rushed through the European Council and European

[37] As the definition in Article 1 constitutes the core of the Framework Decision, I will focus on that in this chapter. There are, however, also other more or less problematic provisions in the text, for

Parliament" (NÍ AOLÁIN 2003:76), but only finally adopted in June 2002, because of parliamentary reserves. As a result, the text in the Framework Decision differs from the one that the EU Commission had initially proposed. Most notably, the definition of terrorism was criticized for violating fundamental rights, for example by the European Parliament (2001b), which managed to change the text of the definition so that increased protection of fundamental rights could be guaranteed.

The provisions violating fundamental rights mainly resulted from the fact that the definition was aimed at covering acts of urban violence, such as protests against G8 summits; Italy especially hoped that anti-globalization demonstrations could be covered in order to blur terrorism with other offences (SAUL 2006:165). However, it would go too far to analyze these changes in detail and I now turn to the deficiencies in human rights protection of the adopted Framework Decision, rather than discussing the minor changes that were made in the process of the adoption.

As the definition in Article 1 of the Framework Decision is the core of the whole text and the other Articles refer to this definition, most concerns are related to this definition. In general, it is said to be too broad, too vague and too extensive, which leads to the problem that it can be used against legitimate democratic expression (NÍ AOLÁIN 2003:79). The International Commission of Jurists (ICJ 2007) has also raised concerns about the wide definition of the Framework's Decision.

I will now first look at those parts of the definition that have been criticized, then describe which human rights could be violated given the definition and then in a last step, analyze in more detail whether the respective human rights provisions are indeed violated.

The definition of terrorism in the Framework Decisions is three-partite, referring to the context of the action, the aim, and then to the specific acts that are committed. The acts covered by the Framework Decision are punished more heavily, than other criminal offences not related to terrorism (BURES 2006:66). The exact wording of the important part, which has been criticized for being in breach with human rights, Article 1(1), reads as follows:

> "Each member state shall take the necessary measures to ensure that the intentional acts referred to below in point (a) to (i), as defined as offences under national law, which,

---

example concerning membership or support of a terrorist group. The whole Framework Decision on Combating Terrorism can be found in Appendix II.

given their nature or context, *may seriously damage a country* or an international organization were committed with the aim of:

- *Seriously intimidating* a population, or
- *Unduly compelling* a Government or international organization to perform or abstain from performing any act, or
- *Seriously destabilizing or destroying* the fundamental political, constitutional, economic or social structures of a country or an international organization, shall be deemed to be terrorist offences (..):

(b) attacks upon the physical integrity of a person; (..)

(d) causing *extensive destruction* to a Government or public facility, a transport system, an infrastructure facility, including an information system, a fixed platform located on the continental shelf, a public place or private property likely to endanger human life or result in *major economic loss* (..)" (Council of the European Union 2002a).[38]

The emphasized expressions have raised most concerns. That is, first the fact that "acts that *may seriously* damage a country or an international organization" fall under the definition of terrorism, in case that they aim at intimidating the population or compelling the government. Apparently, actual damage is not necessary; the possibility that it may happen is sufficient (SAUL 2006:164). It has been claimed that this wording infringes upon the right to freedom of assembly, because demonstrations for instance usually aim at compelling a government and can end up in violent acts.

A second human right that has been claimed to be violated is the principle of legal certainty, which means that "criminal offences must be sufficiently clearly formulated for the individuals to foresee to a reasonable extent the application of the law and to regulate their conduct so as to avoid breach of the law" (ICJ 2007:6).

Due to the vague wording, like "*seriously damage*", "*seriously intimidating*", "*unduly compelling*", "*seriously destabilizing or destroying*", "*extensive destruction*" or "*major economic loss*", this legal certainty seems not to be guaranteed, because it is not clear what exactly a serious damage or a major economic loss is.

I will now look at the two possible violations in more detail.

4.1.2 The Right to Freedom of Assembly

One major criticism is that the offences listed in the definition of terrorism could cover demonstrations and protests and also acts of urban violence[39]. As a result,

[38] Emphasis added. For the complete definition given in the Framework Decision please refer to Chapter 1.1.2 on page 14 of this paper or to Appendix II, where the whole Framework Decision can be found.

[39] See for example NÍ AOLÁIN 2003 or also KRIEGER 2004.

large-scale demonstrations could be forbidden, because they would constitute terrorist acts by definition and the distinction between a demonstrator, a rioter and a terrorist is blurred.

The right to freedom of assembly is enshrined in Article 11 ECHR[40]. In a similar way, the right is also manifested in Article 12 of the 'Charter of Fundamental Rights of the European Union' and in Article 21 ICCPR (European Union 2000; United Nations 1966a). It is thus an internationally acknowledged human right, which should not be undermined.

The definition of terrorism states that

> "(..) offences under national law, which, given their nature or context, may seriously damage a country or an international organization" in case that they aim at "(s)eriously intimidating a population, or (u)nduly compelling a Government or international organization to perform or abstain from performing any act, or (s)eriously destabilizing or destroying the fundamental political, constitutional, economic or social structures of a country or an international organization, shall be deemed to be terrorist offences (..)" (Council of the European Union 2002a).

Of special importance are the offences (b) and (d), which refer to "attacks upon the physical integrity of a person" (b) and "the extensive destruction to a Government or public facility, a transport system, an infrastructure facility, including an information system, a fixed platform located on the continental shelf, a public placc or private property likely to endanger human life or result in major economic loss" (d).

This definition indeed covers large-scale demonstrations and also acts of urban violence, like the riots in the *banlieues* of France's big cities in fall 2005, because these riots seriously intimidated the population, tried to unduly compel the government by extensively destroying public facilitics, infrastructure and private property, endangering human lives and resulting in major economic loss. While such acts are clearly unacceptable and criminal, they are not and should not be considered as terrorist acts. Thus, the agreement gives a kind of counterintuitive definition of terrorism.

Coming back to the demonstrations and the freedom to assembly: the problematic expression in the definition is that it is sufficient if an act "may cause seriously damage to a country or an international organization" and in the past, large-scale demonstrations, such as the G8 summit protests in Genoa 2001, which were planned

[40] The ECHR is provided in Appendix III.

– at least by most participants – as peaceful protests, have – due to some radical individuals or groups within the demonstration – led to damages and destruction. As a result, they would fall under the definition of terrorism and could in the future lead to a prohibition of such demonstrations. Another issue is the expression "given their nature and context", which might widen the scope of terrorist acts, because it can be used to eliminate "the need to prove an intention to intimidate, compel or destabilize" (SAUL 2006:164).

For these reasons, some academics, like FIONNUALA NÍ AOLÁIN (2003:77), claim that the Framework Decision "has the capacity to suppress legitimate public expression or dissent, as well as to act as a means to target unpopular or marginal political views".

In addition, by including fixed platforms on the continental shelf, acts of Greenpeace, such as the occupation of the Brent Spar, could be covered here and with the inclusion of information systems hacking has also become a part of the definition, at least in cases where these acts aim at compelling a government or international organization to perform or abstain from performing any act (Statewatch 2001).

"Attacks upon the physical integrity of a person" have in this respect often been interpreted as implying injury to police during demonstrations (KRIEGER 2004:70).

All these facts reveal the strong impression that the right to peaceful assembly can be suppressed by means of applying this definition. Of course, under certain circumstances the freedom of assembly and association can be restricted according to Article 11 ECHR, but the definition is so indefinite and far-reaching that demonstrations could even be forbidden without sufficient evidence that they might end in extreme violence. This argues for a breach of Article 11 ECHR, because acts that are not criminal in the first place can be covered by the definition and ordinary demonstrators would as a result qualify as terrorists. A second problem is that criminal acts which usually are not understood as being terrorist acts fall under the definition of terrorism, such as acts of urban violence. This is clearly a clash between the protection of human rights and the definition of terrorism.

Opponents of this view, argue that the word "unduly" in the definition serves to exclude demonstrators from it (VENNEMANN 2004:237). In my view, this argument is flawed, because first, it is unclear what exactly unduly means in this respect – this is a matter of interpretation. Second, if some radical groups within a demonstration break out of the peaceful protesting crowd and start committing violent acts, this would most likely be "unduly", because it is an inappropriate means to compel a government or an international organization. But the risk that something like this happens during a demonstration can never be ruled out and this would be enough to be covered by the definition.

VENNEMANN (2004:237) has also proposed to use a high threshold for "major economic loss". However, first there is no defined threshold for "major economic loss" and it is unlikely that one will be agreed. Second, it is impossible to set a clear boundary for this economic loss, especially because some terrorist groups make use of urban violence, such as the ETA, which has pursued a kind of *intifadah* strategy (KRIEGER 2004:71). A too low threshold would therefore lead to an exclusion of these types of terrorist acts.

The problem that remains is that states can set the threshold for their purposes and that they can even make use of rather low thresholds in order to suppress certain groups. Thus, the definition alone could be abused in order to suppress legitimate protest.

The definition is embedded in the framework decision and has to be interpreted in the light of the whole text. The Preamble of the Framework Decision, which can be considered as the guideline for interpretation, states that fundamental rights that are guaranteed in the European Convention of Human Rights, and that the general principles of Community law and the Charter of Fundamental Rights of the EU should also be respected. Direct reference is made to the freedom of assembly and association, and it is said that nothing in the Framework Decision should be interpreted in a way that reduces or restricts fundamental rights (Council of the European Union 2002a:Preamble, §10).

This paragraph, which serves as a guideline for interpretation suggests a restrictive interpretation of the definition and this would lead to an exclusion of demonstrations and other acts that are commonly not perceived as being terrorist.

Further, Article 1(2), which immediately follows the definition of terrorism, provides that

> "(t)his Framework Decision shall not have the effect of altering the obligation to respect fundamental rights and fundamental legal principles as enshrined in Article 6 of the Treaty on European Union."[41]

[41] As explained in Chapter 3, Article 6 TEU requires that the EU respects fundamental rights as enshrined in the ECHR and in the constitutions of the member states.

Thus there is even a second provision, reaffirming the necessity of respecting human rights law when implementing and applying the Framework Decision.

In addition, a declaration has been added to the whole Framework Decision prohibiting the incrimination of persons exercising "their legitimate right to manifest their opinions, even if in the course of the exercise of such right they commit offences" (ICCL 2003:10).

This leads to the conclusion that in the case of a restrictive interpretation and full respect for the Preamble, Article 1(2) and the Additional Statement, human rights are sufficiently protected. However, the mere definition, without these further provisions, is not sufficient to guarantee human rights and could easily be abused in order to suppress certain undesired opinions. Another problem is that the *addendum* is not legally binding and that some states, such as Ireland, have not implemented it (ibid). The Framework Decision thus apparently leaves enough room for abuse and it remains to be seen whether states will make use of these loopholes in the future.

4.1.3 The Principle of Legal Certainty

As the foregoing analysis has already shown, the vague, broad and extensive definition leaves room for interpretation. This impreciseness of used expressions has basically led to a second criticism.

The EU Network of Independent Experts in Fundamental Rights (CFR-CDF 2003:11) has raised concerns that the definition refers to "degrees of seriousness". These "degrees of seriousness" refer to expressions such as "seriously damage", "seriously intimidating" or "seriously destabilizing" in the definition, but terms like "major economic loss" or "unduly compelling" are also somewhat unclear and imprecise and can be interpreted differently: they leave room for an interpretation according to respective needs. The lower the threshold is set, the more groups and individuals could be called "terrorist". Taking into consideration that those groups and individuals fall under special legal treatment, for example they can be subject to unheralded sanctions[42], this could be a serious human rights problem.

The respective human rights principle is the principle of legal certainty, which is enshrined in Article 7 ECHR[43]. Similar provisions on the principles of legality and

[42] See for example Chapter 4.2 on Terrorist Lists.

[43] Please refer to Appendix III for the Convention on Human Rights.

proportionality of criminal offences and penalties are to be found in Article 49 of the Charter of Fundamental Rights of the EU and in Article 15 ICCPR (Council of the European Union 2000, United Nations 1966a).

In essence, this provision is usually interpreted in a way that means "criminal offences must be sufficiently clearly formulated for the individuals to foresee to a reasonable extent the application of the law and to regulate their conduct so as to avoid breach of the law" (ICJ 2007:6). Further, it refers also to retroactivity in the sense that states may not apply criminal law retroactively.

It has been claimed that this definition makes it impossible for the individuals to know for what acts they can be held liable and in what way, because the distinction between different offences are merely described by the gravity of their consequences (CFR-CDF 2003:16), namely the "degree of seriousness" (ibid:11) which can be interpreted differently by everyone.

For this reason, the EU Network of Independent Experts in Fundamental Rights (ibid) and the International Commission of Jurists (ICJ 2007) have found that the breadth of the definition of terrorism breaches the principle of legality.

Additionally, the statement that the Council of the EU added to the final text does not change this assessment:

> "The Council declares that the framework decision on the fight against terrorism covers acts which are considered by all Member States of the European Union as serious infringements of their criminal laws committed by individuals whose objectives constitute a threat to their democratic societies respecting the rule of law and the civilisation upon which these societies are founded. It has to be understood in this sense and cannot be construed so as to argue that the conduct of those who have acted in the interests of preserving or restoring these democratic values, as was notably the case in some Member States during the Second World War, could now be considered as "terrorist acts". Nor can it be construed so as to incriminate on terrorist grounds persons exercising their legitimate right to manifest their opinions, even if in the course of the exercise of such right they commit offences" (ICCL 2003).

At first glance, it seems that the statement recognizes a distinction between terrorism and those who "manifest their opinions" (ibid), even if they commit offences mentioned in the definition without being terrorists. However, since this statement has no legal force, it does not change the general meaning of the Framework

Decision. This means that the states, when implementing the Framework Decision, do not have to incorporate this distinction.[44]

Opponents of the view that the definition breaches Article 7 of the ECHR counter that the principle of legal certainty cannot prohibit the use of terms that are open to interpretation, and that as a result the principle of legal certainty is not violated (VENNEMANN 2004:256). Indeed, the European Court of Human Rights judged in *Müller et al.* in 1988 that "(t)he need to avoid excessive rigidity and to keep pace with changing circumstances means that many laws are inevitably couched in terms which, to a greater or lesser extent, are vague[45]".

This statement of the Court can clearly be interpreted in the sense that the condition of predictability of a law does not require a detailed presentation of all facts that are engaged in criminal liability (DUMITRIU 2004:602).

In addition, as already noted in the analysis of the right to freedom of assembly, the Framework Decision refers directly to the respect for fundamental rights in two provisions, and the Preamble makes special reference to Chapter VI of the Charter of Fundamental Rights of the EU. The principle of legal certainty is part of Chapter VI of this Charter.

As with the right to freedom of assembly, this suggests a restrictive interpretation of the definition and when the definition is interpreted in such a restrictive way, with respect to fundamental rights and high thresholds for the differently vaguely worded expressions, the compliance with Article 7 ECHR could be guaranteed.

However, the way the whole definition is worded makes it a kind of a border case with respect to the principle of legal certainty and it opens – despite the provisions for respecting fundamental rights – a broad margin for interpretation and thus abuse. The way terrorism is defined is not only vague, but extremely vague. The fact that the Framework Decision calls on the states to respect the principle of legal certainty does not make the wording of the definition better understandable or enable one to foresee the application of the law to an adequate extent.

[44] And as already mentioned before, some states, like Ireland, have basically ignored the statement when implementing the Framework Decision (ICCL 2003). See CFR-CDF (2003) for more cases.

4.1.4 Summary

The definition of terrorist offences given in the Framework Decision has evoked two major criticisms, namely that it is in breach with the 'Right to Freedom of Assembly' in Article 11 ECHR, and with the 'Principle of Legal Certainty' in Article 7 ECHR. These human rights concerns result from the vague wording of the definition. Due to the use of broad and vague terms, demonstrators could be covered by the definition of terrorism, which would restrict the right to freedom of assembly. Criminal acts that are not related to terrorism, like urban violence, could also be covered by the definition.

Another problem is that individuals cannot any longer foresee the application of the law to an adequate extent, as required by Article 7 ECHR.

However, because the definition is embedded in the framework of the whole text, the provisions calling on the states to follow their human rights obligations must also be taken into consideration, and actually both the 'Right to Freedom of Assembly' and the 'Principle of Lawfulness' are emphasized. Taking these paragraphs as guidelines for interpretation, proposes a restrictive understanding of the definition. Nevertheless, the vague wording of the Framework Decision makes it difficult to exclude the possibility of human rights violations. The Declaration that has been added to the Framework Decision, which aimed at improving human rights protection, does not change much in this regard because it is without legal binding force and has been completely ignored in some countries.

Experts, such as the International Commission of Jurists or the EU network of independent experts in fundamental rights, as well as non-governmental organizations, such as Statewatch, at least see a breach of Article 7 ECHR.

In sum, I would subscribe to PEERS (2003:243) conclusions on the legal analysis of the Framework Decision. The definition contains "adequate protection of human rights *if* its preamble and statements attached to it are fully applied[46]". Nevertheless he warns that "the ambiguity of the Framework Decision taken by the EU Council make it necessary to keep a close eye on the Union's and its Member States' implementation of the policy because of possible abuses of human rights in certain cases" (ibid).

---

[45] Cited in DUMITRIU 2004:602.

[46] Original emphasis.

4.2 The Lists of Terrorists and Terrorist Organizations

When talking about 'terrorist lists' in the EU, three lists have to be distinguished. There is one UN list, created by the 'Security Council Committee on Al Qaeda and Taliban', which has been merely implemented by the EU, and two lists that the EU has established itself.

In 2001, the Council of the European Union (2001b) provided a list with names of terrorists and terrorist groups in a Common Position, which was implemented with the EC (2001) Regulation 2580 on the same day. Intuitively, one would expect the same list in this latter regulation, but this is not the case. For this reason, there exists a third list, namely the one in the EC Regulation.

These lists aim at freezing all funds and economic resources belonging to natural or legal persons, groups or entities that are named on the list, in order to prevent further terrorist attacks, by depriving them of their financial means.

The problems with all these lists are manifold: the committees decide on adding names in secret meetings, it is not clear by which criteria they add names, persons or groups are not informed about their adding, there is apparently not a real proof needed that a certain person or group is terrorist, it is not clear how persons or groups can be removed from the list and whether they have a right to compensation.

This leads to a number of human rights standards that seem to have been violated. Academics, experts and plaintiffs at the European Courts have specifically mentioned the presumption of innocence, the right to property, the right to a fair hearing and the right to defense as being violated by the lists. In the remainder of this chapter, I will first look at the lists set up by the EU directly, namely those of Common Position 931/2001 and EC Regulation 2580(2001) and then in a next step, analyze the list that the UN has created. This latter list only contains names of individuals, groups and entities that are somehow linked to Al Qaeda, Osama bin Laden or the Taliban. The other two lists identify other individuals and terrorist groups, thus the lists do not overlap. In both assessments, I will take decisions of the European Courts into consideration.

4.2.1 The two Lists set up in 931/2001/CFSP and Regulation EC 2580(2001)

On 27 September 2001, a list of terrorists was established by the 'Council Common Position 2001/931/CFSP on the application of specific measures to combat terrorism', in order to implement the UNSC Resolution 1373(2001). The Common Position regulates that funds, financial assets and economic resources of those people and groups involved in terrorist activities and listed in its annex are to be frozen. In addition, banks and other financial institutions should provide information about those individuals and groups.

The list is drawn up on the basis of information of the competent authorities. These are mainly, but not only, judicial authorities and the list shall be updated at least every six months. Some individuals are also suggested by the UN. The Common Position does not contain any information about the de-listing of names or regarding the exact criteria by which names can be added; it merely says that "precise information and material" shall serve as a basis, however, there is no further clarification on that (Council of the European Union 2001b). These provisions have been criticized by the EU network of independent experts as not being satisfactory (CFR-CDF 2003:43). Moreover, members of the Committee setting up the list acknowledged that some of the decisions were questionable (SCHLAMP 2007:125).

Thus the list contains on the one hand names of groups, entities and individuals that the UN has identified – but not those identified by the Al Qaeda and Taliban Sanctions Committee – and on the other hand, it contains names that the EU has added itself.

Most individuals listed are either of Arabic origin or Spanish ETA activists. The list contains the name, date and city of birth, the terrorist group of which the person is a member, and their passport number. Initially, 29 individuals and 13 organizations were listed; by 2006, the Council of the EU (2006b) had already listed 45 individuals and 48 organizations and networks. The terrorist organizations include, besides Islamist networks, different European ones, like the Real IRA or the ETA and South American and Asian groupings. Thus, the combat against terrorism is directed outwards, but also inwards. The member states support each other in arresting the individuals and groups and in freezing their assets. The first publication of this list evoked protests, because it was not clear on which basis individuals and groups on the list have been chosen. The persons and groups concerned do not have any opportunities to resist against the fact that their name is on this list and it is also not clear how people who have falsely been suspected can be removed (MESSELKEN 2003:15).

In order to implement the Common Position 2001/931/CFSP, including its annex, the European Community Regulation 2580/2001/EC was adopted. This is a normal procedure, however what is interesting is that the list in the annex of the Regulation differs from that in the Common Position. Some authors claim, that his underlines even more that the creation of these lists is not transparent (VENNEMANN 2004:253). Even though it is true that how and why persons and groups are added to the list is unclear, this argument is not correct because the EU has only the power to take unilateral measures against persons and groups acting in third countries (GEHR 2004:82; ADAM 2005:93). For this reason, the list in the Annex of the Regulation EC 2580(2001) is shorter than that of Common Position 2001/931/CFSP: it only contains the names of non-European groups and persons[47].

However, both lists seem to be in breach of several human right standards, as mentioned above. The right to fair hearing, the right to defense, the presumption of innocence, the right to an effective remedy and the right to property have been mentioned in this respect. The first three rights are set forth in Article 6 ECHR. With these two lists, the EU does not comply with any of the paragraphs of Article 6 ECHR: by adding the names of individuals and groups on the list, in non-public meetings, without informing the accused persons and groups, this list is in breach with Article 6(1) ECHR, because the accused are basically judged without being granted the right of a fair hearing. Article 6(2) ECHR is also violated because added persons and groups are prejudged without having been really convicted for a certain crime. Finally, all sub-paragraphs of Article 6(3) are violated because the accused are not informed about their addition to the list.

The right to an effective remedy, Article 13 ECHR is also infringed upon, as there basically is not any effective remedy for the added groups and individuals.[48]

[47] It must be noted that in the annex of the EC Regulation also the Dutch branch of Al Aqsa, the *Stichting Al Aqsa*, is listed, at least in 2005. I could not find out why this inner-European group is on the list. I assume that it could be added, because it is merely a branch of an organization headquartered outside of the EU. The two updated annexes of October 2005 served as a basis for the comparison (Council of the European Union 2005c, European Community 2005) As the annexes of the Regulation does not have to be published obligatory, it is not possible to compare all annexes.

[48] Please refer to Appendix III for the text of the respective Article.

Similar provisions are enshrined in Article 47 and 48 of the Charter of Fundamental Rights of the EU and in Article 14 ICCPR (European Union 2000; United Nations 1966a).

In some cases, it was also claimed that the freedom of assembly and association, Article 11 ECHR, could be violated because once a group has been added to the list, it was officially found as terrorist group and thus restricted in its way to act. However, the Segi Association, which made this claim, only saw this right challenged, but not actually violated[49]. In addition, the right to association and assembly is not an absolute right; therefore, even if it were to a certain extent restricted, it would not necessarily be a breach of this right.

In addition, it has been claimed that the right to property is infringed upon, especially because the freezing of bank accounts and all kinds of funds will continue for an indeterminate time period and not merely for a short period. The accused persons are thus deprived of any income. The right to property is enshrined in the Fundamental Charter of the EU. It was initially not part of the ECHR, but with the Protocol of 1952, it also became part of the ECHR. In addition, the right is enshrined in Article 17 UDHR and it can be considered as part of the 'general principles of EC law'.

The ECHR provision on the right to property provides for restrictions if it is in "public interest". As the fight against terrorism is surely of public interest, one could argue that the restriction on the right to property does not breach this provision.

However, the problem is first, that accused persons are deprived of all their property and they should somehow have enough money to survive and second, the procedure in which the names are added to the list is so dubious that individuals or groups that are not terrorists might be added and as a result falsely be deprived of their property.

A number of cases have been lodged at the European Courts regarding the grounds of this list and some have already been decided[50]. For example, in 2002, after having been added to the list of the Common Position, the *Organisation des Modjahedines du peuple d'Iran,* the People's Mujahidin of Iran, has lodged an application at the European Court of First Instance. The applicant claimed that the Court should annul the Common Positions and the Decisions in which the applicant was added to the terrorist list, declare the lists as inapplicable for the applicant, order the Council to pay the costs of the case and to pay 1 € damage to the applicant.

[49] See below, when case-law on the terror lists is presented.

[50] See Appendix IV for a list of cases and brief summaries.

In its judgment on December 2006, the Court found that the right to fair hearing must be safeguarded by the national authorities, which decide on adding a certain person or group, or if this is initiated by the Council then the Council has the duty to safeguard this right. There is also an obligation to state reasons. Further,

> "(i)n the case of a subsequent decision to freeze funds, observance of the right to a fair hearing similarly requires, first, that the party concerned be informed of the information or material in the file which, in the view of the Council, justifies maintaining it in the disputed lists, and also, where applicable, of any new material referred to in paragraph 125 above and, second, that it must be afforded the opportunity effectively to make known its view on the matter" (European Court of First Instance 2006:§126).

In Conclusion, the Court dismissed the action insofar as it concerned the annulment of the Common Positions, it annulled "in so far as it concerns the applicant, Council Decision 2005/930/EC of 21 December 2005 implementing Article 2(3) of Regulation (EC) No 2580/2001 on specific restrictive measures directed against certain persons and entities with a view to combating terrorism and repealing Decision 2005/848/EC" (ibid). It dismissed the claim for the damages as inadmissible and the Council had to bear its own costs, as well as four fifths of the costs of the applicant and the UK, which supported the Council, also had to bear its own costs (ibid).

Thus, the case was successful for the applicant and the Court has confirmed that the member states and the Council do not respect fundamental rights in a sufficient way. The list does not have to be abolished completely, but the rights of the individuals and groups added should be respected when setting up the list. From a human rights perspective, this case is a success and it confirms the human rights concerns that have been raised.

A number of cases have also been dismissed by the Court, for example a case lodged by the PKK, but several applicants have filed appeals against the judgments at the European Court of Justice. In the case of the PKK, the latter Court has ruled in favor of the applicant and the case was returned to the Court of First Instance. A number of cases have not been decided yet.

An application was also lodged at theEuropean Court of Human Rights. In the case of *Segi and Gestoras pro Amnistía v Council of the EU*[51], the Segi Association, which

[51] The Court has decided to join the two cases. They are very similar and I will only look at the claims of *Segi*.

had been added to the list, but a freezing of bank accounts and assets was not ordered, found:

- the presumption of innocence flouted and a violation of the rights to fair hearing and fair trial (Article 6 ECHR),
- its assets under threat (Article 1 of the 1952 Protocol to the ECHR),
- that the right to freedom of expression had been infringed upon (Article 10 ECHR)
- that the freedom of association was challenged (Article 11 ECHR)
- that the right to judicial remedy did not exist at all (Article 13 ECHR).

The Court dismissed the case on the grounds of Article 34 and 35 §§ 1, 3 and 4 ECHR, mainly because the fundamental rights of the groups were challenged but not actually violated (Article 34), and before lodging a case at the European Court of Human Rights all domestic remedies must have been exhausted (Article 35). However, the Court also found that the circumstances under which the two individual plaintiffs were added to the list was somewhat troublesome (ECrtHR 2003b; Statewatch 2002). The plaintiffs then lodged a case at the European Court of First instance, the case was dismissed and the appeal at the European Court of Justice was also dismissed (European Court of First Instance 2004; European Court of Justice 2007).

Despite the fact that this latter case was rejected, the recent case-law can be considered as success, because in the case of the *People's Mujahidin of Iran* the Court of First Instance has found fundamental rights of the plaintiff violated, and has ruled to remove the group from the list. It remains to be seen what will happen with the pending cases.

In sum, it can be held that Article 6 ECHR and Article 13 ECHR are violated by the way the lists are set up, as listed persons and groups are deprived of their right of fair hearing, fair trial and the presumption of innocence. They do not have any possibility to defend themselves and there is no right to judicial remedy. The Court of First Instance ruled in some cases that the plaintiffs had to be removed from the list and has criticized the way the lists are set up. It is likely that more plaintiffs will have to be removed from the lists and that, resulting from the criticism of the Courts, the EU will make the setting up of the lists more transparent.

4.2.2 The UN List implemented by Regulation EC 881(2002)

On the international level, two different methods of freezing funds exist, one is specifically related to Al Qaeda and the Taliban and existed even before 9/11, the other is a more general obligation for the member states to freeze funds of terrorists and terrorist organizations. This latter method has been implemented by the EU Common position 2001/931/CFSP and the respective Regulation EC 2580(2001), dealt with in the foregoing chapter.

With UNSC Resolution 1333(2000) it was decided that the funds of Osama bin Laden as well as individuals and groups associated with him have to be frozen (United Nations 2000). The UN Committee 1267, also known as 'Al Qaeda and Taliban Sanctions Committee' was charged with the task of setting up a list with names of such associates. Since then, the list has regularly been updated[52].

The Committee decides in non-public sessions on the lists, the criteria on which the listing is based are not public, the listed groups and individuals are neither heard, nor informed and there is no official judicial procedure, so that the concerned cannot call on a review of the decision. Names are listed in an "open outcry" procedure (AREND and HEINZ 2005:18), which means that any person in the Committee can just exclaim a name. In case that within a period of 48 hours no one objects to the listing of the respective person or group, it is added to the list (ibid; STOLL 2006:121). This short time limit makes it almost impossible for members of the Committee to seriously examine a suggestion.

After international criticism, one way of getting de-listed was provided: the concerned persons can address a petition to their government and the government can then bring the request to de-list the concerned to the UNSC[53] (SCHMALENBACH 2006:350). However, this neither gives the affected persons and groups a right to participate and be heard in the review process, nor does it constitute an independent review mechanism. De-listing is only possible with the consent of all governments participating in the Committee (LEHNARDT 2007).

---

52 The last update has been made on 8 June 2007 (United Nations 2007b).

53 This shows a problem of international law in cases where it directly affects individuals: the individuals or groups are directly affected, but as international law is traditionally inter-state law, there are no direct ways for the concerned to act; they rather have to make use of the classical instrument of diplomatic protection offered by states.

UNSC Resolutions are binding. In the case of the EU, it is not directly bound by them, but the EU member states are – and as a result, the list had to be implemented. The EU was thus bound by the Resolution through the member states and implemented it for them[54].

In May 2002, the Council Regulation 881/2002 was finally adopted, updating Council Regulation 467/2001, which has the UN list in its annex. It has been updated regularly.

The main difference between the UN list and the EU list, dealt with in the foregoing part, is that the former contains only names of individuals, groups and entities associated with the Taliban, Osama bin Laden or Al Qaeda. The human rights concerns are basically the same that have also been raised in relation to the EU lists. For example in the *Yusuf* and *Kadi*, cases, the plaintiffs were all listed in the annex of Regulation 467/2001 and sought its annulment on the grounds that it infringed upon their rights to property, to a fair hearing, and to an effective judicial remedy (LEHNARDT 2007). They also claimed that the EU lacked the competence to adopt the regulation.

In its judgment of the *Kadi* and *Yusuf* cases, the Court essentially analyzed the relationship between UNSC resolutions and Community law and found that the SC resolutions took precedence over Community law, as well as in matters related to fundamental rights. "Citing Articles 25, 48(2), 103 of the UN Charter and Article 27 of the Vienna Convention on the Laws of Treaties, the Court concluded that the obligations arising under the Charter prevailed over any other obligation, including the obligation under Community law to respect fundamental rights[55]" (European Court of First Instance 2005; LEHNHARDT 2007).

---

[54] Article 60(1) EC and 301 EC provide that the EC is competent for movement of capital and payments towards third countries. However the implementation of such resolutions is characterized by a relative complex interplay between the national level, the regional level and the international level. But as the purpose of this paper is to analyze the measures taken by the EU in the light of human rights law, it would go too far to analyze in detail whether, how, and why the EC has the competences – or does not have the competences – to implement the UN list on the EU level. It is a matter of fact that the EC has done so and this is what counts for this paper.

[55] Article 25 UNC states that "The Members of the United Nations agree to accept and carry out the decisions of the Security Council in accordance with the present Charter." Article 48 (2) UNC states that "Such decisions shall be carried out by the Members of the United Nations directly and through their action in the appropriate international agencies of which they are members." "Such decisions" refers to the decisions taken by the Security Council. Article 103 UNC reads as follows "In the event of a conflict between the obligations of the Members of the United Nations

The Court goes on with a discussion of *jus cogens* as a higher body of law by which all subjects of international law are bound. If *jus cogens* was violated, there would be grounds for the EC and the member states not to be bound by the UNSC resolution. But the Court found that *jus cogens* was not breached. It dismissed both cases.
Both plaintiffs filed appeal against the judgments at the European Court of Justice in November and December 2005. The cases are still pending[56].
Further cases at the Court of First Instance are pending, for example the case of *Othman v Council of the European Union and the Commission of the European Communities*. In this case the plaintiff sees especially Article 3 ECHR and 8 ECHR violated (European Court of First Instance 2001). These two specific articles have not been mentioned in the other cases.
Article 3 ECHR states that "No one shall be subjected to torture or to inhuman or degrading treatment or punishment." This provision is one of the non-derogable ones in the ECHR. It is part of *jus cogens*. Since the Court has found in the *Yusuf* and *Kadi* cases that *jus cogens* is not violated by the EC regulation implementing the UN list, it is very likely that the Court will not agree with the plaintiff on this point. In addition, it is actually not obvious why he sees himself exposed to torture or inhuman treatment. Moreover, the other plaintiffs and critics of the list have not claimed that Article 3 ECHR is violated. While the list is clearly in breach of some fundamental rights norms, there does not seem to be a breach of the absolute prohibition of torture.
Article 8 ECHR refers to the right to private life[57]. The right to privacy is not absolute. If a restriction is needed to ensure public safety or in order to protect the rights and freedoms of others, it is permitted. Once someone is on the list, he is considered as a terrorist and interference in his private life would be allowed according to the Convention. The problem is thus not Article 8 ECHR, but the procedure of how persons and groups are added to the list, because if that procedure were transparent and legitimate, interference in private life would clearly be allowed. It remains to be seen how the court will decide this case.

---

under the present Charter and their obligations under any other international agreement, their obligations under the present Charter shall prevail."

Article 27 of the Vienna Convention on the law of Treaties regulates that "A party may not invoke the provisions of its internal law as justification for its failure to perform a treaty. This rule is without prejudice to article 46."

[56] Status as of June 17, 2007.

[57] The Article can be found in Appendix III.

Resulting from the different judgments, the list of groups, entities and individuals associated with Al Qaeda and the Taliban is for now legal in the EU – despite the fact that it obviously is in breach of several human rights[58]. The call for annulment of the regulation has so far failed, but there are still appeals pending at the European Court of Justice.

A recent European Court of Human (2007) decision is interesting in this respect. In the *Saramati* case[59], the Court rejects the responsibility of states for measures taken by the UN and stresses the role of the UN in maintaining international peace and security:

> "148. (..) In particular, it is evident from the Preamble, Articles 1, 2 and 24 as well as Chapter VII of the Charter that the primary objective of the UN is the maintenance of international peace and security. While it is equally clear that ensuring respect for human rights represents an important contribution to achieving international peace (see the Preamble to the Convention), the fact remains that the UNSC has primary responsibility, as well as extensive means under Chapter VII, to fulfil this objective, notably through the use of coercive measures.
> 149. In the present case, Chapter VII allowed the UNSC to adopt coercive measures in reaction to an identified conflict considered to threaten peace, namely UNSC Resolution 1244 establishing UNMIK and KFOR. Since operations established by UNSC Resolutions under Chapter VII of the UN Charter are fundamental to the mission of the UN to secure international peace and security and since they rely for their effectiveness on support from member states, the *Convention cannot be interpreted in a manner which would subject the acts and omissions of Contracting Parties which are covered by UNSC Resolutions and occur prior to or in the course of such missions, to the scrutiny of the Court.* To do so would be to interfere with the fulfilment of the UN's key mission in this field including, as argued by certain parties, with the effective conduct of its operations. It would also be tantamount to imposing conditions on the implementation of a UNSC Resolution which were not provided for in the text of the Resolution itself[60]" (ECrtHR 2007).

[58] It would go beyond the scope of this paper to discuss the Court decisions in detail. The decision of the Court in these cases has partly been supported, for example STEINBARTH (2006), but the whole situation has also been discussed in a more critical way, even before the judgments were made (VENNEMANN 2004).

[59] The ECrtHR decided on the admissibility of *Saramati v Germany,France and Norway* in May 2007. The plaintiff was detained by UNMIK police in Kosovo in April 2001, he appealed against a further detention and was released. In July 2001, he was again arrested by UNMIK, by order of a KFOR commander. The detention was extended and KFOR justified it by SC Resolution 1244(1999). The applicant complained under Article 5 ECHR, the right to liberty and security, Article 13 ECHR, the right to an effective remedy, Article 6(1) ECHR, the right to fair trial and Article 1 ECHR, respect for human rights that Germany, Norway and France failed in guaranteeing these rights. The *Saramati* case against Germany was withdrawn, the application against France and Norway was found inadmissible.

[60] Emphasis added.

At first glance, this case seems to reaffirm the statements of the Court of First Instance in the 'terrorist list cases' insofar as UNSC resolutions precede European or domestic law and that for this reason states have to implement them, because the UN relies on the states to implement them – as they are –, otherwise they will not work out.

However, the Court leaves a backdoor open here: by saying that acts and omissions of contracting parties to the Convention that "occur prior to or in the course of such missions" the Court does not rule out that once the mission or operation is over, a discussion according to human rights criteria can take place.

The problem with UNSC resolutions is that if the Court had decided to admit the case now and had, just hypothetically, decided in favor of the applicant, that would have led to an undermining of the UNSC decisions. This could in turn lead to problems with implementing UNSC resolutions in the future and basically the authority of the UN could be undermined. In leaving this door open, the mission of the UN is not endangered, as long as it continues, but human rights law cannot completely be undermined because there is some control possible in the aftermath.

4.2.3 Summary

All three lists are clearly in breach with human rights law, namely Articles 6 and 13 ECHR: the right to fair trial and fair hearing, the presumption of innocence and the right to judicial remedy.

The existence of the list as such does not violate human rights; it is mainly the way it is set up. For the lists established by the EU, the EU can be held liable and there are a number of cases pending at both the Court of First Instance and the Court of Justice. Further, in the case of the People's Mujahidin of Iran for example, the plaintiff was successful and had to be removed from the list.

In order to make the lists conform to human rights standards, the development of binding criteria for the listing of persons and groups should be introduced as well legal protection for those who have been listed. In addition, financial compensation should be granted to those who have been falsely listed and a possibility to restore their personal integrity (AREND and HEINZ 2005:19). These are all rather small steps, but they would make the listing more transparent and lead to compliance with human rights law. An annulment of the lists would not be necessary and they could still serve the aim to identify terrorist persons, groups and entities and to freeze their funds and assets. It remains to be seen whether and what the EU will change with regard to the list, especially after the criticisms of the Court of First Instance.

The situation is more difficult in the case of the UN list, because it is an international obligation to implement UNSC resolutions. Any decision in favor of the applicants at any European Court would undermine the authority of the UN. It is therefore difficult to assess whether the EU can really be held liable for the problems resulting from this list. The Court decisions reject this, but with the decision of the Court of Human Rights in the *Saramati* case, the Court leaves a backdoor for a later evaluation of acts violating human rights and resulting from UNSC resolutions.

4.3 The European Arrest Warrant

The idea of a European Arrest Warrant was already mentioned in the Tampere Conclusions of 1999, in order to abolish the formal extradition procedures. It was however controversial among the member states and the 'Framework Decision on the European Arrest Warrant and the Surrender Procedures between Member States' was only adopted in June 2002 (BURES 2006:61).

The European Arrest Warrant introduces a number of innovations:

- Clear time-limits for the formal extradition procedures;
- Any political involvement of Ministers of Foreign Affairs or Ministers of Justice is excluded, there is merely one judicial decision needed for both states, the requesting and the surrendering state, while traditionally two procedures are required;
- For a list of thirty-two serious offences, the principle of double criminal liability is abolished, among these offences is terrorism. This means that one state can request the extradition of a certain person for some offence that is criminal in the requesting state and it does not matter whether it is also criminal in the extraditing state. The latter accepts the rule of law of the requesting state as binding (HECKER 2006:275). The fact that this is true for thirty-two offences shows that terrorist acts are by no means the only offences concerned.
- Additionally, two reasons for a refusal of extradition are abolished; one of political offence and another of nationality, thus nationals of the surrendering state can be extradited.

The EAW is based on the mutual recognition of the decision of EU member states in criminal law matters.

The Preamble refers to a number of human rights that have to be protected and respected in the application of the EAW and that can lead to a rejection of the surrender: Paragraph 10 regulates that in case of a serious and persistent breach of Articles 6(1) and 7 TEU, the implementation of the EAW can be suspended. Paragraph 13 prohibits extradition if there is a risk of the suspect being subjected to inhuman treatment, torture or the death penalty and paragraph 12 reads as follows:

> "This Framework Decision respects fundamental rights and observes the principles recognised by Article 6 of the Treaty on European Union and reflected in the Charter of Fundamental Rights of the European Union, in particular Chapter VI thereof. Nothing in this Framework Decision may be interpreted as prohibiting refusal to surrender a person for whom a European Arrest Warrant has been issued when there are reasons to believe, on the basis of objective elements, that the said arrest warrant has been issued for the purpose of prosecuting or punishing a person on the grounds of his or her sex, race, religion, ethnic origin, nationality, language, political opinions or sexual orientation, or that that person's position may be prejudiced for any of these reasons" (Council of the European Union 2002b).

Article 1(3) also refers explicitly to Article 6 TEU. A number of specific rights are protected in the operative part of the Framework Decision as well, such as the right to information, translation, counsel and an interpreter, if the person does not agree to extradition, the right to hearing is guaranteed, and a number of other rights are explicitly protected, which shows that the authors of this text tried to protect fundamental rights as extensively as possible. There are also a number of other provisions that can lead to a rejection of extradition or that qualify the surrendering states to only surrender under certain conditions[61].

Another more substantive concern is that 'retransfer' is restricted. For example if someone has committed a criminal act in his own country, and this act is not criminal in their country, the person can be extradited to another country where the act is criminal and can be convicted for it, but because the act is not punishable in the home country, the respective person cannot be retransferred (BLEKXTOON quoted in Den Boer 2006:92-93).

[61] Article 4 provides Grounds for optional non-execution of the European Arrest Warrant and Article 5 provides Guarantees to be given by the issuing member state in particular cases (Council of the European Union 2002b).

Pre-trial detention has also been mentioned as a problem, because accused and extradited persons are usually foreigners in the countries to which they were extradited, they thus do not have any permanent address there. In such cases, many countries allow for detention because there is a high risk of the accused fleeing (AREND and HEINZ 2005: 20).

The main problem with this measure is that criminal law in the different EU countries is not harmonized – fundamental rights enshrined in the basic law of one country might not be the same in another country. In addition, many countries have the prohibition of extradition of nationals as a fundamental right, in Germany this is enshrined in Article 16 of the basic law, the *Grundgesetz*. Regarding criminal law, Spain has, resulting from its experience with the ETA, stricter anti-terrorism laws than other states – a suspect there would be treated differently, and probably more strictly and with a higher penalty than in its own state (DEN BOER 2006:92).

The German Constitutional Court, the *Bundesverfassungsgericht*, judged in 2005 that the Arrest Warrant cannot be implemented in Germany in the way in which the government did it, because the fundamental rights that are guaranteed to the German citizens by the basic law, the *Grundgesetz*, cannot be guaranteed when the EAW is implemented and executed.

A general breach of the rights enshrined in the 'Charter of Fundamental Rights of the EU' or the 'European Convention of Human Rights' is thus not the fundamental rights problem of the EAW, the problem rather results from the different fundamental rights and domestic criminal procedures of the member states. This is a serious problem, but the differences in fundamental rights and criminal law cannot be analyzed here in detail, this is beyond the scope of this paper.

4.4 The EU-US Agreements

Almost immediately after 9/11, the EU and the US intensified their cooperation in the fight against terrorism and the EU has often stressed its deep solidarity with the US. This has led to an institutionalization of contacts between the US and the EU (KNELANGEN 2005). This institutionalization is expressed in the form of three mutual agreements: one agreement on extradition, one on mutual legal assistance and the third on passenger name records. All three agreements have been criticized from a human rights point of view: the extradition treaty because the US imposes and executes the death penalty and the European Convention on Human Rights is usually interpreted in a way that does not allow for extradition to countries having the death penalty, the agreement on mutual legal assistance has been criticized because it is not clear to what extent the US has access to data of European citizens and how the US makes use of this data, and finally the agreement on passenger name records was mainly criticized because the US required an amount of data that seemed neither necessary nor proportionate. In addition, the US has far lower data protection standards than the EU.

4.4.1 The Extradition Treaty

After 9/11, the US had a strong interest in an extradition treaty with the EU, similar to the one between the different EU member states. The problems with such an extradition treaty are quite obvious: the US imposes and practices the death penalty and they have detention camps, most importantly Guantánamo, in which detainees are deprived of their right to fair trial, fair hearing, defense and the principle of *habeas corpus*, which is basically an act of releasing a person from unlawful imprisonment. Detainees are most probably also subject to torture and inhuman treatment.

Extradition to a country imposing the death penalty is not conformable with the Additional Protocol No 13 to the European Convention of Human Rights[62] (Council of Europe 2002b).

This Protocol makes the prohibition of the death penalty an absolute and non-derogable right. This right is guaranteed to all EU citizens and therefore it has been interpreted in a way that also prohibits extradition to countries practicing the death penalty.

Article 2 of the Charter of Fundamental Rights also prohibits the death penalty and Article 19 forbids the extradition to countries where the extradited person would face a serious risk of being condemned to a death penalty (European Union 2000).

[62] Protocol 6 to the ECHR also abolishes the death penalty, however Protocol 13 has been adopted at a later point and goes further by making it an absolute right. All EU member countries and accession countries have to ratify Protocol 13.

In February 2003 (MONAR 2005a:413), an agreement was reached that, according to Article 13, allows for denial of extradition in cases where the death penalty will be imposed or carried out:

> "Where the offence for which extradition is sought is punishable by death under the laws in the requesting State and not punishable by death under the laws in the requested State, the requested State may grant extradition on the condition that the death penalty shall not be imposed on the person sought, or if for procedural reasons such condition cannot be complied with by the requesting State, on condition that the death penalty if imposed shall not be carried out. If the requesting State accepts extradition subject to conditions pursuant to this Article, it shall comply with the conditions. If the requesting State does not accept the conditions, the request for extradition *may* be denied[63]" (Agreement on Extradition between the European Union and the United States of America 2003).

The problem here is that extradition only may be denied, but in fact *is* not denied. This means there is not a clear prohibition in case that the death penalty will be imposed, which is a violation of the absolute – non-derogable – prohibition of the death penalty.

In addition, a clause has been introduced in the Preamble, guaranteeing a fair trial before an impartial tribunal:

> "MINDFUL of the guarantees under their respective legal systems which provide an accused person with the right to a fair trial, including the right to adjudication by an impartial tribunal established pursuant to law" (ibid).

Furthermore, fundamental rights of the individual are in more general terms ensured in the Preamble: "HAVING DUE REGARD for rights of individuals and the rule of law" (ibid).

These provisions shall protect extradited persons from being detained without any fair hearing and trial, for example in Guantánamo, and also in general serve as a protection of fundamental rights.

What are not explicitly mentioned as a reason for refusing extradition are judgements, for example of the European Court of Human Rights, but Article 17(2) can be understood in this sense:

---

[63] Emphasis added.

> "Where the constitutional principles of, or final judicial decisions binding upon, the requested State may pose an impediment to fulfilment of its obligation to extradite, and resolution of the matter is not provided for in this Agreement or the applicable bilateral treaty, consultations shall take place between the requested and requesting States" (ibid).

In sum, the treaty tries to protect fundamental rights and by having direct reference to the right to fair trial and an impartial tribunal, the EU made a big effort in ensuring procedural rights to a large extent. The only problem that remains is the fact that extradition is not explicitly prohibited in cases where the extradited person faces the risk of the death penalty. This is in breach with the European Convention of Human Rights and the Charter of Fundamental Rights.

4.4.2 The Agreement on Mutual Legal Assistance

The Agreement on Mutual Legal Assistance (2003) was signed on the same day when the Agreement on Extradition was concluded. It contains the same protection provisions with regard to fundamental rights that the Extradition treaty comprises, discussed in the foregoing part.

Most notably, the agreement gives US authorities access to bank account information and regulates the creation and work of joint investigative teams. As the US will have access to data of European citizens, the agreement also contains extensive provisions for data protection in Article 9[64].

Even though these provisions are quite extensive and cover a number of data protection issues, they do not fully comply with the rights guaranteed in the EU.

The European Convention of Human Rights contains only a very general provision regarding data protection in Article 8, the right to privacy. However, the EU has had a Data Protection Directive since 1995, in which gathering, processing and disclosure of personal data are regulated. Personal information is any kind of "information relating to an identified or identifiable natural person" (European Community 1995:Article 2)[65].

The Charter of Fundamental Rights of the EU also provides a high level of data protection and will serve as a point of reference here.

[64] The text of Article 9 is provided in Appendix V.

Article 8 of the Charter of Fundamental Rights reads as follows:

> "Protection of personal data
> 1. Everyone has the right to the protection of personal data concerning him or her.
> 2. Such data must be processed fairly for specified purposes and on the basis of the consent of the person concerned or some other legitimate basis laid down by law. Everyone has the right of access to data which has been collected concerning him or her, and the right to have it rectified.
> 3. Compliance with these rules shall be subject to control by an independent authority."

In the mutual agreement, the scope of information exchange is relatively broad: if both states agree, data can be exchanged "for any purpose" (Agreement on Mutual Legal Assistance between the European Union and the United States of America 2003). This would be in breach with §2 Article 8 Charter of Fundamental Rights, because data exchange "for any purpose" is not "fairly for specified purposes", as the Charter requires, and the concerned persons are not asked for their consent.

Further, the Charter guarantees access to data for rectification – it is not obvious that concerned persons have this right, it is not even clear that one will be informed about the fact that data has been exchanged. It is also not regulated how long data can be retained and who exactly has access to it. This is very problematic when one takes into consideration that the US does not have any constitutional right to privacy or data protection and shares the data among different government institutions (KRIEGER 2004).

Another problem is that access to the data by third countries is not regulated at all – overall, the provisions therefore do not effectively protect fundamental rights which are guaranteed to the European citizens with regard to data protection.

4.4.3 The Passenger Name Records

After 9/11, the US passed legislation requiring that air carriers which operate flights to the US, across the US or from the US, have to provide US authorities with electronic access to the data of the reservation and departure control systems, which is called Passenger Name Record. The EU was concerned about the data protection of its citizens and the Commission therefore started negotiations with the US.

[65] On the Council of Europe level, a Convention on the Protection of Personal Data exists.

During these negotiations, of which the European Parliament was only marginally informed, it adopted three critical resolutions and expressed deep concerns about the negotiations[66].

In general however, the US only made minor concessions. Nevertheless, the Commission found that the United States Bureau of Customs and Border Protection, to which the data was to be transferred, provided an adequate level of data protection (European Community 2004b). The Council then decided that an agreement on PNR data can be concluded. On 28 May 2004, the agreement was signed.

The European Parliament applied to the European Court of Justice for annulment of the Council Decision and for annulment of the decision that data protection was adequate.

The Court annulled both decisions in its judgment on 30 May 2006 because the agreement does not fall within the EC, but rather within the EU competences. The Court did not however rule that data protection is violated (European out of Justice 2006).

For now an Interim Agreement is in force, which was signed in October 2006. In early 2007, negotiations for a new agreement started (House of Lords 2007:§78).

The passenger data includes thirty-four items, among them name, address, date and place of birth, credit card numbers, information on travel insurance, seat number, number of luggage and so on. The EU managed to remove sensitive information such as eating habits or ethnicity (AREND and HEINZ 2005:17). The Interim Agreement contains a reference in the Preamble to fundamental rights as ensured in Article 6 TEU (House of Lords 2007).

It is obvious that the agreement does not comply with the standard set out in the Charter on Fundamental Rights. According to Article 8(1), everyone has the right for data protection, however, if one wants to or has to fly to the US, this data protection can no longer be guaranteed, especially as it is today required by US law that PNR

---

[66] The 'resolution on transfer of personal data by airlines in the case of transatlantic flights' in March 2003 and in October 2003 a 'state of negotiations' concerning the same agreement. In these resolutions, the Parliament finds that the US is inadequate to provide the necessary data protection, that it is not necessary for the US to keep the data for more than 6 years and that the number of items required by the US is not necessary and not proportionate. A third resolution was published in March 2004, on the 'draft Commission decision noting the adequate level of protection provided for personal data contained in the Passenger Name Records (PNRs) transferred to the US Bureau of Customs and Border Protection' (European Parliament 2003a, b and 2004).

data is shared with other US agencies (House of Lords 2007:§62). The data thus does not remain in the Bureau of Customs and Border Protection, but can be shared with all other government authorities of the US.

In addition, according to MICHAEL CHERTOFF (2007:118), Secretary of the Department of Homeland Security, the US retains the data for forty years. It might even be accessible for third countries. Article 8 §§2 and 3 are also not respected here: as the data is shared within the US, perhaps even with third countries, it is not "processed fairly for specified purposes", it is not possible to access the data and to rectify it and there is no independent authority controlling the application of the rules – because the data is no longer within the EU, but in the US. The US moreover has far lower data protection standards than the EU (KRIEGER 2004).

The Data Protection Directive of the EU actually does not allow for transfer of data, in case that an appropriate protection to personal data cannot be granted – this is certainly the case with the PNR agreement. At the end of July 2007, the agreement will expire. The EU will try to cut down the information exchanged to the US. It remains to be seen whether the US will agree to such a limitation. According to MICHEAL CHERTOFF (2007), this is rather unlikely: the US wants to at least keep the thirty-four exchanged items, wants to share them within the US with different authorities, and wants to retain the data for decades.

4.4.4 Summary

In sum, the three agreements are all – to a greater or lesser extent – in breach with fundamental rights guaranteed to EU citizens: the extradition agreement does not strictly prohibit extradition to the US, even if the risk of the imposition and execution of death penalty exists.

The agreement on mutual legal assistance does not protect data to a sufficient extent, concerned persons do not have a right to access the data or to rectify it, and it is not certain which authorities have access to the data and whether it will be submitted to third states. The information that is exchanged also does not comply with the rule that it should be "processed fairly for specified purposes", as with consent of the states, "any purpose" can qualify for exchange.

Finally, the PNR agreement also violates the data protection provisions enshrined in the Charter of Fundamental Rights: the data is shared within the US with different agencies, it is not clear that third countries do not have access to it, the concerned persons do not have any access to the data and therefore do not have the possibility for rectification and there is also not an independent controlling authority.

4.5 Data Protection

With regard to data protection within the EU, the Directive on Data Retention, formally adopted on 15 March 2006, is of major importance. The fact that biometric data has to be included in passports has also been criticized. A number of new measures related to data protection issues are on the way of adoption these days, for example the expansion of the Prüm Treaty to the whole EU[67].

The problem with stored biometric data is that it can be used in connection with surveillance of public spaces, which is already the case in some countries and cities, to trace movements of individuals (AREND and HEINZ 2005:17). While this is surely useful in order to pursue terrorists, it can easily be abused and would then violate Article 8 ECHR[68], as the respect for private life is not guaranteed and restrictions on this right are only allowed if they are in interest of national security or for public safety.

Another problem, related to biometric data is that some systems have 20% margins of error, which makes the systems as such rather unreliable.

Apart from biometric data, the data retention directive has been adopted, which requires phone and internet providers to retain data of their customers for at least six months, and at most two years. Most essentially the source of communications as well as the destination shall be identified, as well as the date, time and duration of communications, the communication device and the location insofar as mobile equipment is concerned. The retention is limited to traffic, rather than content, but still, this is sufficient to lay open all private and business contacts of an individual. The retained data will be made accessible for national authorities in serious criminal cases; a judicial warrant is not necessary and there is not a list of crimes that qualify for making the data available (European Community 2006).

This means that the state is quite powerful in monitoring and controlling the citizens and as the crimes are not specified, the data retention might lead to abuses. Taking

[67] See Chapter 2.3

[68] See Appendix III.

into consideration how broad the EU definition of terrorism is, data could be used in order to control groups or people organizing, for example, large-scale demonstrations.

In order to ensure the highest protection, parts of Article 8 ECHR are cited in the Preamble and it is further said that

> "Because retention of data has proven to be such a necessary and effective investigative tool for law enforcement in investigations in several Member States and in particular into serious cases such as organized crime and terrorism, it is therefore necessary to ensure availability of retained data to law enforcement for a certain period of time under the conditions provided for in the present Directive. The adoption of an instrument on retention of data is therefore a necessary measure in accordance with the requirements of Article 8 of the European Convention on Human Rights." (European Community 2006)

In general, Article 8 ECHR is respected and guaranteed here. It might be a problem that there is not a specified list of crimes that qualify for the request of data from a service provider and maybe the time period of retention is too long, but there is no general access of government authorities to the data. This is only the case if the concerned person is most likely involved in serious crimes, and in such cases, interference is allowed by Article 8 ECHR: interference is justified in the interest of public safety and national security. Thus, Article 8 ECHR is not violated here, but it might be abused, resulting *inter alia* from the broad definition of terrorist offences.

Apart from the European Convention of Human Rights, there is a 'Data Protection Telecommunication Directive', restricting states in gathering data from telecommunication systems, however, also in this directive, reasons of national security allow for exceptions (European Community 1997). Furthermore, the European Court of Human Rights extensively protected the privacy of European citizens in the past[69]. Yet terrorism is clearly a threat to national security, allowing for limitations on this right.

However, taking into consideration that data of the whole population and not just of suspects are gathered, there should be strict regulations controlling the circumstances under which government authorities should get access to it.

---

[69] See Krieger (2004).

4.6 Summary

In sum the definition of terrorism given in the Framework Decision is vaguely worded and makes it difficult to exclude violations of fundamental rights resulting from it. In particular, the freedom of assembly and the principle of legal certainty have been mentioned in this respect. In general, the definition provides an adequate protection of human rights if the provisions in the preamble and the additional statement are fully applied. If not, it offers a number of loopholes that can be used to restrict fundamental rights.

The three terrorist lists are clearly in breach of human rights law, because the presumption of innocence, the right to hearing and fair trial and the right to judicial remedy are violated. In case of the UN list, the EU has so far not been held liable, because it merely implemented a UNSC resolution, but with the EU lists, plaintiffs complaining about the EU have partly been successful.

The European Arrest Warrant seems to pose a challenge to fundamental rights enshrined in the national constitutions, but is not in breach with European human rights protection.

The three agreements between the EU and the US have also been analyzed and it is striking that all the three violate fundamental rights law of the EU: the extradition treaty does not strictly prohibit extradition, if the concerned person faces the risk of being punished by the death penalty and the agreement on mutual legal assistance as well as the one on PNR does not comply with data protection standards, guaranteed to EU citizens.

The fact that biometric data has to be included in passports leads to some problems with the right of privacy, as well as the data retention directive, while they are both not clearly in breach of the right to privacy, they can be abused by national authorities in order to control specific groups or persons, which then would lead to a violation of the right to privacy.

Conclusions

This book has sought to answer the questions of how the EU has reacted to the 'new' threat of terrorism after 9/11 and how these reactions relate to human rights law.
I have proposed two possible answers to this latter question:
a) the EU complies with fundamental human rights law in their actions; or
b) the EU does not comply with human rights law in certain respects.
The analysis of the EU reactions has confirmed the second possible outcome: the EU does not comply with human rights law in certain respects.
Most importantly, the description of the European reactions to terrorism has suggested five elements in the EU's fight against terrorism that have been criticized by expert networks, the European and national Parliaments, and non-governmental organizations for not meeting the human rights standards.
These five reactions are the definition of terrorism in the 'Framework Decision on Combating Terrorism', the three terrorist lists in the EU, established with Common Position 931/2001/CFSP, Regulation EC 2580(2001) and Regulation 881(2002), the European Arrest Warrant, the close EU-US cooperation and the different agreements resulting from it – on extradition, on mutual legal assistance and on passenger name records – and finally, there have been data protection related issues, in particular the data retention directive.
Closer scrutiny of these five criticized EU reactions in the light of human rights law has shown that the core of the EU's fight against terrorism, the definition laid down in the 'Framework Decision on Combating Terrorism', is indeed highly questionable: even though the Framework Decision contains human rights provisions, the definition is so vaguely worded that it can be abused by the states when implementing it and as a result it can lead to human rights violations. The 'Right to Freedom of Assembly', enshrined in Article 11 ECHR and the 'Principle of Legal Certainty', Article 7 ECHR are especially endangered.
The three terror lists, two of which are established by the EU itself and the third one is set up by the UN and merely implemented, are also in breach with human rights law. Whereas the existence of such lists is actually not a problem, the way how they are set up is the problem. Persons and groups are listed in secret meetings, without even being informed. Resulting from this procedure, the right to fair hearing and trial and the presumption of innocence are violated, which are enshrined in Article 6

ECHR. In addition, the accused are deprived of their 'Right to Judicial Remedy', Article 13 ECHR. The multiplicity of applications related to these 'terror lists' lodged at the European Courts, and the fact that in some cases the Court has harshly criticized the procedure of setting up the lists, underline these problems. Many cases are still pending, but there have so far also been few cases in which the applicants were successful.

The European Arrest Warrant was the third measure under scrutiny, it actually does not violate written law at the EU level, but it conflicts with fundamental rights enshrined in the basic law of member states. This is a serious problem, but beyond the scope of this paper. The Arrest Warrant however – which has been established for a list of thirty-two offences – exemplifies how the fight against terrorism has been used in order to enforce measures which are not confined to terrorism, but embrace a number of different crimes.

The close EU-US cooperation has led to basically three agreements, which all entail certain problems. This is actually not surprising, because the US has been suspected and accused of violating human rights and restricting civil liberties in countering terrorism since 9/11. The EU has managed to include a number of human rights safeguards in the agreements, which actually has to be positively acknowledged. Nonetheless, they are not far-reaching enough to ensure the rights that EU citizens are guaranteed: extradition when the death penalty might be imposed is not fully prohibited, which is a breach of Protocol 13 ECHR, and the two other agreements on data protection and passenger name records are both connected to data protection problems. Data protection standards in the US are far lower than in the EU, and if the data of EU citizens is treated according to US law in the US then the EU data protection, as set forth in Article 8 of the Charter of Fundamental Rights of the EU, is not guaranteed.

Data protection is also an issue within the EU. So far a directive on the retention of data has been adopted; further biometric data and in the future also fingerprints have to be included in passports. In addition, a number of new measures are in the pipeline: a common Criminal Record, extended cooperation of the intelligence services, a new Schengen Information System, the expansion of the Prüm Treaty and a number of other measures.

While these measures and proposals are not clearly in breach of human rights law, they involve a number of data protection issues and lead to a closer control and scrutiny of EU citizens and immigrants. This threatens the right to privacy, enshrined in the European Convention on Human Rights and the Charter of Fundamental Rights of the EU. Furthermore, this development is alarming as it might end in a kind of "Big Brother" Europe, where citizens are monitored by the states and the EU in an extensive way (DEN BOER 2006). With regard to this problem, it might be useful to give more power and control capabilities to the European Parliament and the Courts (KNELANGEN 2006:162).

In sum, within the EU human rights and fundamental freedoms have been violated in the fight against terrorism. This is not really surprising, because terrorism is a severe threat to security and the "relationship between human rights protection and the needs of the state in times of crisis has always been involved in delicate balancing" (NÍ AOLÁIN 2003:63). Nevertheless, human rights should not be sacrificed for the right to security (HAARSCHER 2006).

The measures on EU level in general do not seem to go as far as those of the US – the EU has not been accused of setting up secret detention camps or for supporting extraordinary renditions – quite the contrary, the EU has tried to uncover the CIA flights and the secret detention incidents in Council of Europe states quite extensively. This is a positive sign. Further, the EU has not enacted measures violating *jus cogens*, but has rather tried to include a number of human rights safeguards in the decisions. Taking into consideration the relation between the overall number of measures in the fight against terrorism – more than 200 – and the elements that have been criticized from a human rights point of view, shows that the majority of EU reactions to terrorism respects human rights in a sufficient way.

However there are also some alarming developments. Already in April 2007, Germany's Interior Minister proposed to make use of information gained by intelligence services of countries that are known for using torture: as long as one does not know for sure that methods of torture were applied, the information should be used (SCHÄUBLE 2007). As already mentioned in Chapter 2, Charles Clarke proposed to lower the threshold for extradition after the 2005 attacks in London. These issues have been rejected so far, but after the thwarted terrorist attacks in London in June 2007 and the attack on the Glasgow airport in Scotland, also in late June 2007, new discussions on the topic have started. It remains to be seen how the EU reacts to these new incidents.

Since the battle against terrorism is also understood as fight for human rights and the origins of terrorism are, at least partly, related to the infringement of human rights, the fight against terrorism should be in accordance with the body of law that it wants to protect (SEIBERT-FOHR 2004). Otherwise, it can create "a spiral of terrorist acts and counter-measures" (VON SCHORLEMER 2003:274).

To conclude with JOSCHKA FISCHER's (2003) speech, the "unconditional commitment of the Western democracies to their own fundamental values - freedom, human rights, tolerance, democracy, the rule of law and the social market economy" should be a cornerstone of the fight against terrorism. Rather than sacrificing human rights in the fight against terrorism, the EU should stick to these achievements and spread them to the rest of the world: "Positive globalization is the real strategic response to the deadly challenge of a new totalitarianism" (ibid).

Bibliography

ADAM, Alexandre. 2005. *La Lutte contre le Terrorisme. Étude comparative Union européenne – États Unis*. Paris: L'Harmattan.

AGREEMENT ON EXTRADITION BETWEEN THE EUROPEAN UNION AND THE UNITED STATES OF AMERICA. 2003. Washington, 25 June 2003. Retrieved May 24, 2007(http://eur-lex.europa.eu/LexUriServ/site/en/oj/2003/l_181/l_18120030719en00270033.pdf).

AGREEMENT ON MUTUAL LEGAL ASSISTANCE BETWEEN THE EUROPEAN UNION AND THE UNITED STATES OF AMERICA. 2003. Washington, 25 June 2003. Retrieved May 24, 2007 (http://europa.eu.int/eur-lex/pri/en/oj/dat/2003/l_181/l_18120030719en00340042.pdf).

AMNESTY INTERNATIONAL GERMANY. 1977. Annual Report. Retrieved May 10, 2007 (http://www2.amnesty.de/internet/deall.nsf/51a43250d61caccfc1256aa1003d7d38/20228301f58a36b6c1256b6d004aabe1?OpenDocument).

ANNAN, KOFI. 2003 "Statement on a Special Meeting of the Security Council's Counter-Terrorism Committee with International, Regional, and Sub-Regional Organizations." New York. 6 March 2003. Printed in Kielsgard, Mark D. 2006. "A Human Rights Approach to Counter-Terrorism." *California Western International Law Journal* 36/2:249-302. Also available at (http://www.unhchr.ch/terrorism/index.html).

APARICIO, SONIA. 2004. "11-M Masacre en Madrid. El mayor Atentado de la Historia de España." *ElMundo.es* – Online version of El Mundo. Retrieved May 19, 2007 (http://www.elmundo.es/documentos/2004/03/espana/atentados11m/hechos.html).

ARCHICK, KRISTIN. 2003. "Europe and Counter-Terrorism: Strengthening Police and Judicial Cooperation." Pp. 1-34 in *Europe and Counterterrorism*. New York: Nova Science Publishers.

AREND, JAN-MICHAEL and WOLFGANG S. HEINZ. 2005. *The International Fight Against Terrorism and the Protection of Human Rights*. Berlin: Deutsches Institut für Menschenrechte.

ARNOLD, ROBERTA. 2006. "Human Rights in times of Terrorism." *Zeitschrift für ausländisches öffentliches Recht und Völkerrecht (ZaöRV)* 66/2: 297-319.

BAEHR, PETER R. 1999. *Human Rights. Universality in Practice*. New York: St. Martin's Press.

BEDERMAN, DAVID J. 2002. "Counterintuiting Countermeasures." *The American Journal of International Law* 96/4:817-832.

BENYON, JOHN, LYNNE TURNBULL, ANDREW WILLIS, RACHEL WOODWARD and ADRIAN BECK. 1993. *Police Cooperation in Europe: An Investigation*. Leicester: University of Leicester, Centre for the Study of Public Order.

BOTHE, MICHAEL. 2003. "Terrorism and the Legality of Pre-emptive Force." *European Journal of International Law* 14/2:227-240.

BOURLOYANNIS-VRAILAS, CHRISTIANE. 2004. "United Nations Human Rights Standards as Framework Conditions for Anti-Terrorist Measures." Pp. 13-25 in *Anti-Terrorist Measures and Human Rights*. Edited by Wolfgang Benedek and Alice Yotopoulos-Marangopoulos. Leiden: Martin Nijhoff Publishers.

BROOMHALL, BRUCE. 2004. "State Actors in an International Definition of Terrorism from a Human Rights Perspective." *Case Western Reserve Journal of International Law* 36:2-3:421-441.

BUNDESVERFASSUNGSGERICHT. 2005. 2 BvR 2236/04 0f 18. July 2005, Absatz-Nr. (1-201), Retrieved May 18, 2007 (http://www.bverfg.de/entscheidungen/rs20050718_2bvr223604.html).

BURES, OLDRICH. 2006 "EU Counterterrorism Policy: A Paper Tiger?" *Terrorism and Political Violence* 18/1:57-78.

BYMAN, DANIEL L. 2003. "Al-Qaeda as an Adversary: Do We Understand Our Enemy?" *World Politics* 56/1:139-163.

CFR-CDF. 2003. E.U. Network of Independent Experts in Fundamental Rights. "The Balance between Freedom and Security in the Response by the European Union and its Member States to the Terrorist Threats." Retrieved June 8, 2007
(http://ec.europa.eu/justice_home/cfr_cdf/doc/obs_thematique_en.pdf).

CHARNEY, JONATHAN I. 2001. "The Use of Force Against Terrorism in International Law." *American Journal of International Law* 95/4:835-839.

CHERTOFF, MICHAEL. 2007. "Ein Schrei der Empörung." Interview with Michael Chertoff conducted by Georg Mascolo. *Der Spiegel* 24/2007: 118-120.

CLARKE, CHARLES. 2005. *Speech to the European Parliament*. Strasbourg 7 September 2005. Retrieved May 27, 2007
(http://www.eu2005.gov.uk/servlet/Front?pagename=OpenMarket/Xcelerate/ShowPage&c=Page&cid=1107293561746&a=KArticle&aid=1125559979691).

CLEMONS, STEVEN, ROHAN GUNARATNA, URSULA MÜLLER and GEORG MASCOLO. 2005. "Al Qaeda in Europe: Today's Battlefield." Pp. 42-60 in *Al Qaeda Now. Understanding Today's Terrorists*. Edited by Karen J. Greenberg. New York: Cambridge University Press.

CLUB OF MADRID. 2005. "The Madrid Agenda: International Summit on Democracy, Terrorism and Security." 8-11 March 2005.
Retrieved April 6, 2007 (http://english.safe-democracy.org/agenda/the-madrid-agenda.html).

COUNCIL ACT. 1995. "Summary of the Council Act of 10 March 1995 drawing up the Convention on Simplified Extradition Procedure between Member States."
Retrieved May 16, 2007 (http://europa.eu/scadplus/leg/en/lvb/l14015a.htm).

COUNCIL ACT 1996. "Summary of the Council Act of 27 September 1996 drawing up the Convention relating to extradition between the Member States of the European Union." Retrieved May 16, 2007 (http://europa.eu/scadplus/leg/en/lvb/l14015b.htm).

COUNCIL OF EUROPE. 1961. "European Social Charter." CETS No. 035. Turin, 18 October 1961.
Retrieved May 30, 2007 (http://conventions.coe.int/Treaty/EN/Treaties/Html/035.htm).

COUNCIL OF EUROPE. 1977. "European Convention on the Suppression of Terrorism." CETS No. 90. Strasbourg, 27 January 1977.
Retrieved April 7, 2007 (http://conventions.coe.int/Treaty/en/Treaties/Html/090.htm).

COUNCIL OF EUROPE. 2002a. "Guidelines on human rights and the fight against terrorism." Adopted by the Committee of Ministers on 11 July 2002 on the 804th meeting of the Minister's Deputies. Retrieved June 2, 2007
(http://www1.umn.edu/humanrts/instree/HR%20and%20the%20fight%20against%20terrorism.pdf).

COUNCIL OF EUROPE. 2002b. Protocol No. 13 to the Convention for the Protection of Human Rights and Fundamental Freedoms, concerning the abolition of the death penalty in all circumstances. Vilnius, 3.May.2002.
Retrieved June 20, 2007 (http://conventions.coe.int/Treaty/en/Treaties/Html/187.htm).

COUNCIL OF EUROPE. 2003a. "Protocol amending the European Convention on the Suppression of Terrorism." CETS No. 190. Strasbourg, 15 May 2003.
Retrieved April 7, 2007 (http://conventions.coe.int/Treaty/EN/Treaties/Html/190.htm).

COUNCIL OF EUROPE. 2003b. "Convention for the Protection of Human Rights and Fundamental Freedoms." Rome, 4 November 1950. With the Amendment of Protocol Number 11 and the Protocols Nos. 1, 4, 6, 7, 12 and 13. Registry of the European Court of Human Rights September 2003.
Retrieved April 29, 2007. (http://www.echr.coe.int/NR/rdonlyres/D5CC24A7-DC13-4318-B457-5C9014916D7A/0/EnglishAnglais.pdf).

COUNCIL OF EUROPE. 2005a. "Council of Europe Convention on the Prevention of Terrorism." CETS No. 196. Warsaw, 16 May 2005.
Retrieved April 8, 2007 (http://conventions.coe.int/Treaty/en/Treaties/Html/196.htm).

COUNCIL OF EUROPE. 2005b. "Council of Europe Convention on Laundering, Search, Seizure and Confiscation of the Proceeds from Crime and on Financing Terrorism." CETS No. 198. Warsaw 16 May 2005.
Retrieved May 27, 2007 (http://conventions.coe.int/Treaty/en/Treaties/Html/198.htm).

COUNCIL OF EUROPE. 2006. "Dates of ratification of the European Convention on Human Rights and Additional Protocols." Last update: 26/06/2006. Retrieved June 30, 2007 (http://www.echr.coe.int/ECHR/EN/Header/Basic+Texts/Basic+Texts/Dates+of+ratification+of+the+European+Convention+on+Human+Rights+and+Additional+Protocols/).

COUNCIL OF EUROPE. 2007a. "European Social Charter (revised)". CETS No. 163. Status of Ratification as of 24 April 2007. Retrieved May 30, 2007 (http://conventions.coe.int/Treaty/Commun/ChercheSig.asp?NT=163&CM=8&DF=4/24/2007&CL=ENG).

COUNCIL OF EUROPE. 2007b. "List of Declarations made with respect to treaty No. 090: European Convention on the Suppression of Terrorism." Status as of 9 June 2007.
Retrieved June 16, 2007
(http://conventions.coe.int/Treaty/Commun/ListeDeclarations.asp?NT=090&CM=8&DF=5/16/2007&CL=ENG&VL=1).

COUNCIL OF THE EUROPEAN UNION. 2001a. "2001/930/CFSP Council Common Position of 27 December 2001 on combating terrorism" Retrieved May 20, 2007
(http://europa.eu.int/eur-lex/lex/LexUriServ/LexUriServ.do?uri=CELEX:32001E0930:EN:HTML).

COUNCIL OF THE EUROPEAN UNION. 2001b. "2001/931/CFSP Council Common Position of 27 December 2001 on the application of specific measures to combat terrorism." Retrieved May 20, 2007 (http://eur-lex.europa.eu/LexUriServ/site/en/oj/2001/l_344/l_34420011228en00930096.pdf).

COUNCIL OF THE EUROPEAN UNION. 2001c. "Council Framework of 26 June 2001 on money laundering, the identification, tracing, freezing, seizing and confiscation of instrumentalities and the proceeds of crime." (2001/500/JHA). Retrieved June 16, 2007 (http://eur-lex.europa.eu/LexUriServ/site/en/oj/2001/l_182/l_18220010705en00010002.pdf).

COUNCIL OF THE EUROPEAN UNION. 2002a. "Council Framework Decision of June 13, 2002 on combating terrorism." (2002/475/JHA). Retrieved April 7, 2007 (http://europa.eu.int/eur-lex/pri/en/oj/dat/2002/l_164/l_16420020622en00030007.pdf).

COUNCIL OF THE EUROPEAN UNION. 2002b. "Council Framework Decision of 13 June 2002 on the European Arrest Warrant and the surrender procedures between member states." (2002/584/JHA). Retrieved May 20, 2007
(http://europa.eu.int/eur-lex/pri/en/oj/dat/2002/l_190/l_19020020718en00010018.pdf).

COUNCIL OF THE EUROPEAN UNION. 2002c. "Council Framework Decision of 13 June 2002 on joint investigation teams." (2002/465/JHA). Retrieved May 19, 2007 (http://eur-lex.europa.eu/smartapi/cgi/sga_doc?smartapi!celexapi!prod!CELEXnumdoc&lg=EN&numdoc=32002F0465&model=guichett).

COUNCIL OF THE EUROPEAN UNION. 2002d. "Council Decision 2003/48/JHA of 19 December 2002 on the implementation of specific measures for police and judicial cooperation to combat terrorism in accordance with Article 4 of Common Position 2001/931/CFSP."
Retrieved May 24, 2007
(http://eur-lex.europa.eu/LexUriServ/site/en/oj/2003/l_016/l_01620030122en00680070.pdf).

COUNCIL OF THE EUROPEAN UNION. 2005a. "European Union counter-terrorism Strategy." 30 November 2005.
Retrieved May 27, 2007 (http://register.consilium.eu.int/pdf/en/05/st14/st14469-re04.en05.pdf).

COUNCIL OF THE EUROPEAN UNION. 2005b. "Council Decision 2005/876/JHA of 21 November 2005 on the exchange of information extracted from the criminal record."
Retrieved June7, 2007 (http://europa.eu/scadplus/leg/en/lvb/l14500.htm).

COUNCIL OF THE EUROPEAN UNION. 2005c. "Council Common Position 2005/725/CFSP of 17 October 2005 updating Common Position 2001/931/CFSP on the application of specific measures to combat terrorism and repealing Common Position 2005/427/CFSP." Retrieved June 10, 2007 (http://eur-lex.europa.eu/LexUriServ/site/en/oj/2005/l_272/l_27220051018en00280032.pdf).

COUNCIL OF THE EUROPEAN UNION. 2006a. "Council Framework Decision on the European Evidence Warrant." 11235/06. Brussels 10 July 2006.
Retrieved June 8, 2007. (http://register.consilium.europa.eu/pdf/en/06/st11/st11235.en06.pdf).

COUNCIL OF THE EUROPEAN UNION. 2006b. "Council Common Position 2006/380/CFSP of 29 May 2006 updating Common Position 931/2001/CFSP on the application of specific measures to combat terrorism and repealing Common Position 2006/231/CFSP." Retrieved May 17, 2007 (http://eur-lex.europa.eu/LexUriServ/site/en/oj/2006/l_144/l_14420060531en00250029.pdf).

CUMIN, DAVID. 2004. "Tentative de definition du terrorisme à partir du 'jus in bello'." *RSC: Revue de Science Criminelle et de Droit Pénal Comparé* 1:11-30.

DARBY, JOSEPH J. 2005. "Self Defense in Public International Law: the Doctrine of Pre-emption and Its Discontents." Pp. 29-34 in *Internationale Gemeinschaft und Menschenrechte. Festschrift für Georg Ress zum 70. Geburtstag am 21. Januar 2005.* Edited by Roland Bieber, Jürgen Bröhmer, Christian Calliess, Christine Langenfeld, Stefan Weber and Joachim Wolf. Köln: Carl Heymans.

DEN BOER, MONICA. 2006. "Fusing the Fragments. Challenges for EU Internal Security Governance on Terrorism." Pp. 83-111 in *International Terrorism. A European Response to a Global Threat?* Edited by Dieter Mahncke and Jörg Monar. Brussels: Peter Lang.

DENNINGER, ERHARD. 2002. "Zur rechtsstaatlichen Problematik des Terrorismusbekämpfungsgesetzes." Pp.28-31 in *Menschenrechtliche Erfordernisse bei der Bekämpfung des Terrorismus. Bericht und Beiträge zu einem Arbeitsgespräch am 19. April 2002 im Französisischen Dom, Berlin Mitte – Dokumentation.* Berlin: Deutsches Institut für Menschenrechte.

DIMITRIJEVIC, VOJIN. 2003. "Terrorism and Human Rights after 2001." Pp. 603-620 in *Human rights and criminal justice for the downtrodden: Essays in Honour of Asbjorn Eide.* Edited by Morten Bergsmo. Leiden: Martin Nijhoff Publishers.

DUGARD, JOHN. 2005. "The Problem of the Definition of Terrorism in International Law." Pp. 187-205 in *September 11, 2001: A Turning Point in International and Domestic Law?* Edited by Paul Eden and Thérèse O'Donnell. Ardsley: Transnational Publishers.

DUMITRIU, EUGENIA. 2004. "The E.U.'s Definition of Terrorism: The Council Framework Decision on Combating Terrorism." *German Law Journal* 5/5: 585-602.

EATON, MARTIN. 2004. "Human Rights Standards and Framework Conditions for Anti-Terrorist Measures. European Standards and Procedures." Pp. 27-31 in *Anti-Terrorist Measures and Human Rights.* Edited by Wolfgang Benedek and Alice Yotopoulos-Marangopoulos. Leiden: Martin Nijhoff Publishers.

EUROPEAN COMMISSION. 2004a. MEMO/04/63 of the European Commission. "Existing legislative instruments relevant to the fight against terrorism, and draft measures already on the Council table." Brussels, 18 March 2004.
Retrieved May 24, 2007
(http://europa.eu/rapid/pressReleasesAction.do?reference=MEMO/04/63&format=HTML&aged=0&language=EN&guiLanguage=en#file.tmp_Foot_3).

EUROPEAN COMMISSION. 2004b. MEMO/04/66 of the European Commission. "European Commission action paper in response to the terrorist attacks on Madrid." Brussels, 18 March 2004. Retrieved May 24, 2007.
(http://europa.eu/rapid/pressReleasesAction.do?reference=MEMO/04/66&format=HTML&aged=1&language=EN&guiLanguage=fr).

EUROPEAN COMMISSION. 2005. "The Hague Programme – Ten Priorities for the next five years." Brussels 10 May 2005. Retrieved May 27, 2007
(http://ec.europa.eu/justice_home/news/information_dossiers/the_hague_priorities/index_en.htm).

EUROPEAN COMMISSION. 2007. "Free movement of people calls for increased cross-border police co-operation." Retrieved June 13, 2007
(http://ec.europa.eu/justice_home/fsj/police/schengen/fsj_police_schengen_en.htm).

EUROPEAN COMMISSION AND COUNCIL. 1999. "Action Plan of the Council and the Commission on how best to implement the provisions of the Treaty of Amsterdam on the creation of an area of freedom, security and justice." Text adopted by the Justice and Home Affairs Council of 3 December 1998. Retrieved May 16, 2007
(http://eur-lex.europa.eu/LexUriServ/site/en/oj/1999/c_019/c_01919990123en00010015.pdf).

EUROPEAN COMMUNITY. 1995. "Directive 95/46/EC of the European Parliament and of the Council of 24 October 1995 on the protection of individuals with regard to the processing of personal data and on the free movement of such data." Retrieved June 30, 2007 (http://eur-lex.europa.eu/smartapi/cgi/sga_doc?smartapi!celexapi!prod!CELEXnumdoc&lg=EN&numdoc=31995L0046&model=guichett).

EUROPEAN COMMUNITY 1997. "Directive 97/66/EC of the European Parliament and of the Council of 15 December 1997 concerning the processing of personal data and the protection of privacy in the telecommunications sector." Retrieved June 27, 2007
(http://eur-lex.europa.eu/pri/en/oj/dat/1998/l_024/l_02419980130en00010008.pdf).

EUROPEAN COMMUNITY. 2000. "Council Regulation (EC) No 337/2000 of 14 February 2000 concerning a flight ban and a freeze of funds and other financial resources in respect of the Taliban of Afghanistan." Retrieved May 24, 2007
(http://eur-lex.europa.eu/LexUriServ/site/en/oj/2000/l_043/l_04320000216en00010011.pdf).

EUROPEAN COMMUNITY. 2001. "Council Regulation (EC) No 2580/2001 of 27 December 2001 on specific restrictive measures directed against certain persons and entities with a view to combating terrorism." Retrieved May, 21, 2007
(http://eur-lex.europa.eu/smartapi/cgi/sga_doc?smartapi!celexapi!prod!CELEXnumdoc&lg=EN&numdoc=32001R2580&model=guichett).

EUROPEAN COMMUNITY 2002. "Council Regulation 881/2002 of 27 May 2002 imposing certain specific restrictive measures directed against certain persons and entities associated with Usama bin Laden, the Al Qaida network, and the Taliban, and repealing Council Regulation (EC) No 467/2001 prohibiting the export of certain goods and services to Afghanistan, strengthening the flight ban and extending the freeze of funds and other financial resources in respect of the Taliban of Afghanistan." Retrieved May 21, 2007
(http://europa.eu.int/eur-lex/pri/de/oj/dat/2002/l_139/l_13920020529de00090022.pdf).

EUROPEAN COMMUNITY. 2004a. "Council Regulation (EC) No 2007/2004 of 26 October 2004 establishing a European Agency for the Management of Operational Cooperation at the External Borders of the Member States of the European Union" Retrieved May 24, 2007 (http://eur-lex.europa.eu/Notice.do?val=391764:cs&lang=de&list=391764:cs,&pos=1&page=1&nbl=1&pgs=10&hwords=European%20Agency%20for%20the%20Management%20of%20Operational%20Cooperation%20at%20the%20External%20Borders~).

EUROPEAN COMMUNITY. 2004b. "2004/535/EC: Commission Decision of 14 May 2004 on the adequate protection of personal data contained in the Passenger Name Record of air passengers transferred to the United States' Bureau of Customs and Border Protection." Retrieved June 30, 2007 (http://eur-lex.europa.eu/LexUriServ/LexUriServ.do?uri=CELEX:32004D0535:EN:HTML).

EUROPEAN COMMUNITY. 2005. "Council Decision of 17 October 2005 implementing Article 2(3) of Regulation (EC) No 2580/2001 on specific restrictive measures directed against certain persons and entities with a view to combating terrorism and repealing Decision 2005/428/CFSP. 2005/722/EC." Retrieved June 10, 2007 (http://eur-lex.europa.eu/Notice.do?mode=dbl&lang=en&ihmlang=en&lng1=en,de&lng2=cs,da,de,el,en,es,et,fi,fr,hu,it,lt,lv,nl,pl,pt,sk,sl,sv,&val=413234:cs&page=).

EUROPEAN COMMUNITY. 2006. "Directive 2006/24/EC of the European Parliament and of the Council of 15 March 2006 on the retention of data generated or processed in connection with the provision of publicly available electronic communications services or public communications networks and amending directive 2002/58/EC." Retrieved June 8, 2007 (http://www.ispai.ie/DR%20as%20published%20OJ%2013-04-06.pdf).

EUROPEAN COUNCIL. 1995. La Gomera Declaration of the Council of the European Union in the Conclusions of the Madrid European Council. Madrid15 and 16 December 1995. Retrieved May 16, 2007. (http://www.europarl.europa.eu/summits/mad2_en.htm#annex3).

EUROPEAN COUNCIL. 1999. Presidency Conclusions. Tampere, 15 and 16 October 1999. Retrieved May 16, 2007 (http://www.europarl.europa.eu/summits/tam_en.htm).

EUROPEAN COUNCIL. 2001. Conclusions and Plan of Actions of the Extraordinary European Council Meeting on 21 September 2001. Retrieved May 13, 2007 (http://www.consilium.europa.eu/ueDocs/cms_Data/docs/pressData/en/ec/140.en.pdf).

EUROPEAN COUNCIL. 2004. "Declaration on Combating Terrorism." Brussels, 25 March 2004. Retrieved May 27, 2007 (http://ue.eu.int/ueDocs/cms_Data/docs/pressData/en/ec/79637.pdf).

EUROPEAN COURT OF FIRST INSTANCE. 2001. "Action brought on 17 December 2001 by Omar Mohamed Othman against the Council of the European Union and the Commission of the European Communities". Case T-318/01. Pending Case. Retrieved June 20, 2007 (http://europa.eu.int/eur-lex/pri/en/oj/dat/2002/c_068/c_06820020316en00130014.pdf).

EUROPEAN COURT OF FIRST INSTANCE. 2004. "Order of the Court of First Instance (Second Chamber). 7 June 2004. Segi, Araitz Zubimendi Izaga and Aritza Galarraga v Council of the European Union." Case T-338/02. Retrieved June 19, 2007 (http://curia.europa.eu/jurisp/cgi-bin/form.pl?lang=en&Submit=Submit&docor=docor&numaff=338%2F02&datefs=&datefe=&nomusuel=&domaine=&mots=&resmax=100).

EUROPEAN COURT OF FIRST INSTANCE. 2005. "Judgment of the Court of First Instance (Second Chamber, Extended Composition). 21 September 2005. Ahmed Ali Yusuf, Al Barakaat International Foundation v Council of the European Union and Commission of the European Communities." Case T-306/01 R. Joined with case T-315/01 Kadi v Council and Commission. Retrieved June 14, 2007 (http://curia.europa.eu/jurisp/cgi-bin/form.pl?lang=en&Submit=Rechercher&alldocs=alldocs&docj=docj&docop=docop&docor=docor&docjo=docjo&numaff=T-306/01&datefs=&datefe=&nomusuel=&domaine=&mots=&resmax=100).

EUROPEAN COURT OF FIRST INSTANCE. 2006. "Judgment of the Court of First Instance (Second Chamber). 12 December 2006. Organisation des Modjahedines du people d'Iran v Council of the European Union." Case T-228/02. Retrieved June 3, 2007 (http://eur-lex.europa.eu/LexUriServ/LexUriServ.do?uri=CELEX:62002A0228:EN:HTML).

EUROPEAN COURT OF JUSTICE. 1970. "Judgment of the Court of 17 December 1970. Internationale Handelsgesellschaft mbH v Einfuhr- und Vorratsstelle für Getreide und Futtermittel." Case C-11/70. Retrieved June 10, 2007 (http://eur-lex.europa.eu/LexUriServ/LexUriServ.do?uri=CELEX:61970J0011:EN:NOT).

EUROPEAN COURT OF JUSTICE. 1974. "Judgment of the Court of 14 May 1974. J. Nold, Kohlen- und Baustoffgroßhandlung v Commission of the European Communities." Case C-4/73. Retrieved June 10, 2007 (http://eur-lex.europa.eu/LexUriServ/LexUriServ.do?uri=CELEX:61973J0004:EN:NOT).

EUROPEAN COURT OF JUSTICE. 1984. "Judgment of the Court of 10 July 1984. Regina v Kent Kirk." Case C-63/83. Retrieved June 29. 2007 (http://eur-lex.europa.eu/smartapi/cgi/sga_doc?smartapi!celexplus!prod!CELEXnumdoc&numdoc=61983J0063&lg=en).

EUROPEAN COURT OF JUSTICE. 1992. "Judgment of the Court of 5 October 1994. X v Commission of the European Communities." C-404/92P. Retrieved June 29, 2007 (http://eur-lex.europa.eu/smartapi/cgi/sga_doc?smartapi!celexplus!prod!CELEXnumdoc&numdoc=692J0404&lg=EN).

EUROPEAN COURT OF JUSTICE. 2006. "Judgment of the Court of 30 May 2006. European Parliament v Council of the European Communities and European Parliament v Commission of the European Communities." Joined Cases C-317/04 and C-318/04. Retrieved June 10, 2007 (http: //curia.europa.eu/jurisp/cgi-bin/gettext.pl?where=&lang=en&num=79939469C19040317&doc=T&ouvert=T&seance=ARRET).

EUROPEAN COURT OF JUSTICE. 2007. "Judgment of the Court of 27 February 2007. Appeal under Article 56 of the Statute of the Court of Justice lodged at the Court on 17 August 2004. Gestoras Pro Amnistía, Juan Mari Olano Olano, Julen Zelarain Errasti v Council of the European Union and Segi, Araitz Zubimendi Azaga, Aritza Galarraga v Council of the European Union." C-354/04 P and 355/04 P. Retrieved June 20, 2007 (http://www.curia.europa.eu/en/actu/communiques/cp07/aff/cp070016en.pdf).

EUROPEAN COURT OF HUMAN RIGHTS. 2003a. "Call for European Union to accede to European Convention on Human Rights". Press release issued by the Registrar. 28 February 2003. Retrieved May 9, 2007. (http://www.echr.coe.int/eng/Press/2003/jan/Pressconference2003.htm).

EUROPEAN COURT OF HUMAN RIGHTS. 2003b. "Third Section. Annual Activity Report 2002." Retrieved June 29, 2007 (http://www.echr.coe.int/NR/rdonlyres/0FFA1EA7-78E7-40FB-A28F-10D28DA9592E/0/Section3.pdf).

EUROPEAN COURT OF HUMAN RIGHTS. 2006. "European Court of Human Rights Statistics 2006."
Retrieved May 29, 2007 (http://www.echr.coe.int/NR/rdonlyres/5211CDBA-8208-47DE-A9CA-AE8B8FD13872/0/stats2006.pdf).

EUROPEAN COURT OF HUMAN RIGHTS. 2007. "Grand Chamber Decision as to the Admissibility of Application no. 71412/01 by Agim Behrami and Bekir Behrami against France and Application no. 78166/01 by Ruzhdi Saramati against France, Germany and Norway." Retrieved June 18, 2007 (http://cmiskp.echr.coe.int/tkp197/viewhbkm.asp?sessionId=10349038&skin=hudoc-en&action=html&table=F69A27FD8FB86142BF01C1166DEA398649&key=62605&highlight=).

EUROPEAN PARLIAMENT. 2001a. Committee on Citizens' Freedoms and Rights, Justice and Home Affairs. Rapporteur Graham R. Watson. "Report on the Role of the European Union in Combating Terrorism." 5 July 2001. Retrieved May 17, 2007 (http://www.europarl.europa.eu/sides/getDoc.do?pubRef=-//EP//NONSGML+REPORT+A5-2001-0273+0+DOC+PDF+V0//EN).

EUROPEAN PARLIAMENT. 2001b. Committee on Citizens' Freedoms and Rights, Justice and Home Affairs. Rapporteur Graham R. Watson. "Report on the Commission proposal for a Council framework decision on combating terrorism and on the Commission proposal for a Council framework decision on the European arrest warrant and the surrender procedures between the Member States." Retrieved Mai 17, 2007 (http://www.europarl.europa.eu/sides/getDoc.do?type=REPORT&reference=A5-2001-0397&language=EN&mode=XML).

EUROPEAN PARLIAMENT. 2003a. "European Parliament Resolution on Transfer of personal Data by Airlines in the Case of transatlantic Flights." P5 TA (2003) 0097. March 2003. Retrieved May 24, 2007 (http://www.europarl.europa.eu/sides/getDoc.do?pubRef=-//EP//TEXT+TA+P5-TA-2003-0097+0+DOC+XML+V0//EN).

EUROPEAN PARLIAMENT. 2003b."European Parliament Resolution on Transfer of personal Data by Airlines in the Case of transatlantic Flights: State of Negotiations with the USA." P5TA(2003)0429. October 2003. Retrieved May 24, 2007 (http://www.europarl.europa.eu/sides/getDoc.do?pubRef=-//EP//TEXT+TA+P5-TA-2003-0429+0+DOC+XML+V0//EN).

EUROPEAN PARLIAMENT. 2004. "European Parliament Resolution on the Draft Commission Decision noting the adequate Level of Protection provided for Personal Data contained in the Passenger Name Records (PNRs) transferred to the US Bureau of Customs and Border Protection (2004/2011(INI))." P5 TA (2004)0245. March 2004. Retrieved May 24, 2007 (http://www.europarl.europa.eu/sides/getDoc.do?pubRef=-//EP//TEXT+TA+P5-TA-2004-0245+0+DOC+XML+V0//EN).

EUROPEAN PARLIAMENT 2007a. "EU visa information system to help prevent visa shopping." Press Release (Justice and Home Affairs) on 7 June 2007. Retrieved June 12, 2007 (http://www.europarl.europa.eu/news/expert/infopress_page/019-7569-157-06-23-902-20070606IPR07543-06-06-2007-2007-false/default_en.htm).

EUROPEAN PARLIAMENT. 2007b. "Prüm Treaty will allow EU27 to exchange DNA data to fight crime." Press Release (Justice and Home Affairs) on 7 June 2007. Retrieved June, 12, 2007 (http://www.europarl.europa.eu/news/expert/infopress_page/019-7568-157-06-23-902-20070606IPR07542-06-06-2007-2007-false/default_en.htm).

EUROPEAN UNION. 2000. "Charter of Fundamental Rights of the European Union." Retrieved June 1, 2007 (http://www.europarl.europa.eu/charter/pdf/text_en.pdf).

EUROPEAN UNION. 2001a. "Declaration of the European Union and Conclusions." Special Council Meeting, 12 September 2001. Retrieved May 19, 2007 (http://ec.europa.eu/external_relations/gac/12_09_01.htm).

EUROPEAN UNION. 2001b."Joint Declaration by the Heads of State and Government of the European Union, the President of the European Parliament, the President of the European Commission, and the High Representative for the Common Foreign and Security Policy on the September 11 attacks on the US." 14 September 2001. Retrieved May 24, 2007 (http://www.europa-eu-un.org/articles/en/article_46_en.htm).

FALLOWS, JAMES, PETER BERGEN, BRUCE HOFFMAN and STEVEN SIMON. 2005. "Al Qaeda Then and Now." Pp. 3-26 in *Al Qaeda Now. Understanding Today's Terrorists.* Edited by Karen J. Greenberg. New York: Cambridge University Press.

FISCHER, JOSCHKA. 2003. "Europe and the Future of the Transatlantic Relations." Speech at Princeton University on 19 November 2003. Retrieved May 14, 2007 (http://www.germany.info/relaunch/politics/speeches/112003.html).

FLETCHER, GEORGE P. 2006. "The Indefinable Concept of Terrorism." *Journal of International Criminal Justice* 4/5:894-911.

FRANCK, THOMAS M. 2001. "Terrorism and the Right of Self-Defense." *The American Journal of International Law* 95/4:839-843.

GAJA, GIORGIO.2002. "The Attack on the World Trade Center. Legal Responses. In What Sense was There an "Armed Attack"?" *European Journal of International Law – Discussion Forum.* Retrieved May 3, 2007 (http://www.ejil.org/forum_WTC/ny-gaja.html).

GAL-OR, NOEMI. 1985. *International Cooperation to Suppress Terrorism.* London: Croom Helm.

GANOR, BOAZ. 1998. "Defining Terrorism: Is One Man's Terrorist Another Man's Freedom Fighter?" International Institute for Counter-Terrorism.Retrieved April 6, 2007 (http://ictconference.org/var/119/17070-Def%20Terrorism%20by%20Dr.%20Boaz%20Ganor.pdf).

GEHR, WALTER. 2004. "The European Union Approach to Measures against Terrorism." Pp. 79-92 in *Anti-Terrorist Measures and Human Rights*. Edited by Wolfgang Benedek and Alice Yotopoulos-Marangopoulos. Leiden: Martin Nijhoff Publishers.

GENEVA CONVENTION. 1949. "Convention (IV) relative to the Protection of Civilian Persons in Time of War." Geneva, 12 August 1949. Retrieved April 30, 2007 (http://www.icrc.org/ihl.nsf/7c4d08d9b287a42141256739003e636b/6756482d86146898c125641e004aa3c5).

GENEVA CONVENTION. 1977. "Protocol Additional to the Geneva Conventions of 12 August 1949, and relating to the Protection of Victims of International Armed Conflicts (Protocol I)." 8 June 1977. Retrieved April 30, 2007 (http://www.icrc.org/ihl.nsf/7c4d08d9b287a42141256739003e636b/f6c8b9fee14a77fdc125641e0052b079).

GENEVA CONVENTION. 1977. "Protocol Additional to the Geneva Conventions of 12 August 1949, and relating to the Protection of Victims of Non-International Armed Conflicts (Protocol II)." 8 June 1977. Retrieved April 30, 2007 (http://www.icrc.org/ihl.nsf/7c4d08d9b287a42141256739003e636b/d67c3971bcff1c10c125641e0052b545).

GOLDER, BEN AND GEORGE WILLIAMS. 2004. "What is 'Terrorism'?: Problems of Legal Definition." *University of New South Wales Law Journal* 27/2:270-295.

GRANT, CHARLES. 2002. "The Eleventh of September and beyond: The Impact on the European Union." Pp. 135-153 in *Superterrorism: Policy Responses*. Edited by Lawrence Freedman. Oxford: Blackwell Publishing Ltd.

GRAY, CHRISTINE. 2005. "A new war for a new century? The Use of Force against Terrorism after September 11, 2001." Pp. 97-125 in *September 11, 2001: A Turning Point in International and Domestic Law?* Edited by Paul Eden and Thérèse O'Donnell. Ardsley: Transnational Publishers.

GREGORY, FRANK. 2005. "The EU's Response to 9/11: A Case Study of Institutional Roles and Policy Processes with Special Reference to Issues of Accountability and Human Rights." *Terrorism and Political Violence* 17/1&2:105-123.

GUILLAUME, GILBERT. 2004. "Terrorism and International Law." *The International and Comparative Law Quarterly* 53/3:537-548.

GUNARATNA, ROHAN. 2002. *Inside Al Qaeda*. New York: Columbia University Press.

HAARSCHER, GUY. 2006. "Balancing Security and Freedom in an Age of Terror." Pp. 129-149 in *International Terrorism. A European Response to a Global Threat?* Edited by Dieter Mahncke and Jörg Monar. Brussels: Peter Lang.

HECKER, JAN. 2006. "Die Europäisierung der inneren Sicherheit." *Die Öffentliche Verwaltung* 59/7:273-280.

HEINZ, WOLFGANG S. 2007. *Terrorismusbekämpfung und Menschenrechtsschutz in Europa. Examplarische Fragestellungen 2005/2006.* Berlin: Deutsches Institut für Menschenrechte.

HERMANN, RAINER. 2004. "Das Terrornetzwerk al-Qaida: Vom nahöstlichen zum internationalen Terrorismus." Pp. 71-98 in *Islamismus und terroristische Gewalt.* Edited by Reinhard Möller. Würzburg: Ergon Verlag.

HOFFMAN, BRUCE. 2001. *Terrorismus – der unerklärte Krieg. Neue Gefahren politischer Gewalt.* Frankfurt am Main: Fischer.

HOUSE OF COMMONS. 2004. Select Committee on European Scrutiny. Twenty-First Report. "Exchange of information and cooperation concerning terrorist offences." Retrieved June 2, 2007 (http://www.publications.parliament.uk/pa/cm200304/cmselect/cmeuleg/42-xxi/4209.htm).

HOUSE OF COMMONS. 2005. "Report of the official account of the Bombings in London on 7th July 2005." 11 May 2006. Retrieved May 26, 2007. (http://www.official-documents.gov.uk/document/hc0506/hc10/1087/1087.pdf).

HOUSE OF LORDS. 2004. European Union Committee. "Twenty-Third Report."
Retrieved June, 2, 2007
(http://www.publications.parliament.uk/pa/ld200304/ldselect/ldeucom/138/13802.htm).

HOUSE OF LORDS. 2007. European Union Committee. "Twenty-First Report of Session 2006-2007. The EU/US Passenger Name Record Agreement." Retrieved June 20. 2007
(http://www.publications.parliament.uk/pa/ld200607/ldselect/ldeucom/108/108.pdf).

HUMAN RIGHTS WATCH. 2005. "Statement on U.S: Secret Detention Facilities in Europe." November 2005. Retrieved May 27, 2007 (http://hrw.org/english/docs/2005/11/07/usint11995.htm).

ICCL. 2003. Irish Council on Civil Liberties. ICCL Briefing Paper. "Human Rights Compatibility of the Criminal Justice (Terrorist Offences) Bill 2002." April 2003. Retrieved June 10, 2007
(http://www.iccl.ie/DB_Data/publications/Human%20Rights%20Compatibility%20of%20the%20Criminal%20Justice%20(Terrorist%20Offences)%20Bill%202002.pdf).

ICJ. 2005. International Commission of Jurists. "The Berlin Declaration." *Human Rights Quarterly* 27/1:350-356.

ICJ. 2007. International Commission of Jurists. "Response to the European Commission Consultation on Inciting, Aiding or Abetting Terrorist Offences." Retrieved June 9, 2007 (http://www.icj.org/IMG/EC_Questionaire_final.pdf).

ILC. 2001. International Law Commission. Draft Articles on the "Responsibility of states for internationally wrongful acts". Retrieved April 26, 2007
(http://untreaty.un.org/ilc/texts/instruments/english/draft%20articles/9_6_2001.pdf).

INTERNATIONAL COURT OF JUSTICE. 1986. "Case concerning the military and paramilitary activities in and against Nicaragua (Nicaragua v. United States of America) Merits. Judgment of 27 June 1986." Retrieved April 26, 2007
(http://www.icj-cij.org/docket/index.php?sum=367&code=nus&p1=3&p2=3&case=70&k=66&p3=5).

JENNINGS, ROBERT Y. 1938. "The Caroline and McLeod Cases." *American Journal of International Law* 32/1:82-99.

KAHL, MARTIN. 2006. "Die EU und der Kampf gegen den Terrorismus – die schwierige Balance zwischen Sicherheit und Freiheit." *Sicherheit und Frieden* 24/3:123-128.

KEOHANE, DANIEL. 2005. *The EU and Counter-Terrorism*. London: Centre for European Reform.

KEPEL, GILLES and JEAN-PIERRE MILELLI. 2006. *Al Qaida. Texte des Terrors*. Edited and commented by Gilles Kepel and Jean-Pierre Milelli. München: Piper Verlag.

KLEINE, MAREIKE. 2004. *Die Reaktion der EU auf den 11. September*. Münster: Lit Verlag.

KNELANGEN, WILHELM. 2005. "Die Europäische Union und die Bekämpfung des Terrorismus." Pp. 403-414 in *Jahrbuch Öffentliche Sicherheit 2004/2005*. Edited by Martin H.W. Möllers and Robert Chr. Van Ooyen. Frankfurt am Main: Verlag für Polizeiwissenschaft.

KNELANGEN, WILHELM. 2006. "Die innen- und justizpolitische Zusammenarbeit der EU und die Bekämpfung des Terrorismus." Pp. 140-162 in *Die Europäische Union im Kampf gegen den Terrorismus: Sicherheit vs. Freiheit?*Edited by Erwin Müller and Patricia Schneider.Baden-Baden: Nomos Verlagsgesellschaft.

KRIEGER, HEIKE. 2004. "Limitations on Privacy, Freedom of Press, Opinion and Assembly as a Means of Fighting Terrorism." Pp. 51-71 in *Terrorism as a Challenge for National and International Law Security versus Liberty?* Edited by Volker Röben, Frank Schorkopf, Silja Vöneky and Christian Walter. Berlin et al: Springer Verlag.

KURTH CRONIN, Audrey. 2006. "How al-Qaida ends. The Decline and Demise of Terrorist Groups." *International Security* 31/1: 7-48.

LAQUEUR, WALTER. 2003. *No End to War: Terrorism in the Twenty-First Century*. London: Continuum International Publishing Group.

LAQUEUR WALTER. 2004. *Voices of Terror. Manifestos, Writing and Manuals of Al Qaeda, Hamas and other Terrorists from around the World and throughout the Ages*. New York: Reed Press.

LAVALLE, ROBERTO. 2007. "A Politicized and Poorly Conceived Notion Crying Out for Clarification: The Alleged Need for a Universally Agreed Definition of Terrorism." *Zeitschrift für ausländisches Öffentliches Recht und Völkerrecht (ZaÖRV)* 67/1: 89-117.

LEHNARDT, CHIA. 2007. "European Court Rules on UN and EU Terrorist Suspect Blacklists." *ASIL Insight*. 11/1. Retrieved June 20. 2007 (http://www.asil.org/insights/2007/01/insights070131.html).

MAHNCKE, DIETER. 2006. "Introduction." Pp. 13-22 in *International Terrorism. A European Response to a Global Threat?* Edited by Dieter Mahncke and Jörg Monar. Brussels: Peter Lang.

MALLOY, MICHAEL P. 2004. "Was bedeutet Terrorismus?" *The Transnational Lawyer* 17/1: 39-50.

MÉGRET, FRÉDÉRIC. 2002. "'War'? Legal Semantics and the Move to Violence." *European Journal of International Law* 13/2: 1-38.

MERLOS, ALFONSO. 2006. *Al Qaeda. Raíces y metas del terror global.* Madrid: Biblioteca Nueva.

MESSELKEN, DANIEL. 2003. *Europas Antiterrorismus-Politik. Entstehung, Entwicklung, Perspektiven.* Berlin: Berliner Transformationszentrum für Transatlantische Sicherheit (BITS).

MONAR, JÖRG. 2005a. "The European Union and the Challenge of September 11, 2001: Potential and Limits of a 'new' actor in the fight against international terrorism." Pp. 387-418 in *September 11, 2001: A Turning Point in International and Domestic Law?* Edited by Paul Eden and Thérèse O'Donnell. Ardsley: Transnational Publishers.

MONAR, JÖRG. 2005b. "Anti-terrorism law and policy: the case of the European Union." Pp. 425-452 in *Global Anti-Terrorism Law and Policy.* Edited by Michael Hor, Victor V. Ramraj and Kent Roach. Cambridge: Cambridge University Press.

MÜLLER, ERWIN AND PATRICIA SCHNEIDER (eds) 2006. *Die Europäische Union im Kampf gegen den Terrorismus: Sicherheit vs. Freiheit?* Baden-Baden: Nomos Verlagsgesellschaft.

MURPHY, JOHN F. 1989. "Defining international terrorism." *Israel Yearbook on Human Rights*:13-37.

MUSHARBASH, YASSIN. 2006. *Die neue Al-Qaida. Innenansichten eines lernenden Terrornetzwerks.* Köln: Kiepenheuer und Witsch Verlag.

NATO 1949. North Atlantic Treaty Organization. "The North Atlantic Treaty." Washington, 4 April 1949. Retrieved April 28, 2007. (http://www.nato.int/docu/basictxt/treaty.htm).

NATO 2001. North Atlantic Treaty Organization. "Decision of the NATO of September 12, 2001." Retrieved April 28, 2007 (http://www.nato.int/terrorism/five.htm).

NEUHOLD, HANSPETER. 2006. "International Terrorism. Definitions, Challenges and Responses." Pp. 23-46 in *International Terrorism. A European Response to a Global Threat?* Edited by Dieter Mahncke and Jörg Monar. Brussels: Peter Lang.

NÍ AOLÁIN, FIONNUALA. 2003. "Balancing Human Rights: International Legal Responses to Terrorism in the Wake of September 11." Israel Yearbook on Human Rights 33:63-84.

NILSSON, HANS G. 2005. "European and Japanese Responses to September 11 – A Comment." Pp. 447-452 in *September 11, 2001: A Turning Point in International and Domestic Law?* Edited by Paul Eden and Thérèse O'Donnell. Ardsley: Transnational Publishers.

NILSSON, HANS G. 2006. "The EU Action Plan on Combating Terrorism. Assessment and Perspectives." Pp. 73-81 in *International Terrorism. A European Response to a Global Threat?* Edited by Dieter Mahncke and Jörg Monar. Brussels: Peter Lang.

OHCHR. 2007a. Office of the High Commissioner for Human Rights. International Covenant on Civil and Political Rights: Ratification Process. New York, 16 December 1966. Last Update 19 April 2007. Retrieved May 29, 2007 (http://www.ohchr.org/english/countries/ratification/4.htm)

OHCHR. 2007b. Office of the High Commissioner for Human Rights. International Covenant on Economic, Social and Cultural Rights: Ratification Process. New York, 16 December 1966. Last Update 19 April 2007.
Retrieved May 29, 2007 (http://www.ohchr.org/english/countries/ratification/3.htm).

PEERS, STEVE. 2003. "EU Responses to Terrorism." *International and Comparative Law Quarterly* 52/1:227-244.

POKEMPNER, DINAH. 2002. "Terrorism and Human Rights. The Legal Framework." Pp. 19-29 in *Terrorism and International Law: Challenges and Responses. Contributions presented at the "Meeting of independent experts on Terrorism and International Law: Challenges and Responses. Complementary Nature of Human Rights, Law, International Humanitarian Law and Refugee Law" and the "Seminar on International Humanitarian Law and Terrorism"*. San Remo: International Institute of Humanitarian Law.

RATNER, STEVEN R. 2002. "Jus ad Bellum and Jus ad Bello after September 11." *The American Journal of International Law* 96/4:905-921.

REES, WYN. 2006. "International Cooperation in Counter-Terrorism. The Translantic Dimension and Beyond." Pp. 113-127 in *International Terrorism. A European Response to a Global Threat?* Edited by Dieter Mahncke and Jörg Monar. Brussels: Peter Lang.

RICHARDSON, LOUISE. 2000. "Terrorists as Transnational Actors." Pp. 209-219 in *The Future of Terrorism*. Edited by Max Taylor and John Horgan. London: Frank Cass Publishers.

ROSAND, ERIC. 2003. "Security Council's Resolution 1373, the Counter-Terrorism Committee, and the Fight against Terrorism." *The American Journal of International Law* 97/2:333-341.

SAGHI, OMAR. 2006. "Osama bin Laden. Volkstribun im Medienzeitalter." Pp. 25-54 in *Al Qaida. Texte des Terrors*. Edited by Gilles Kepel and Jean-Pierre Milelli. München: Piper Verlag.

SAUL, BEN. 2005. "Attempts to define 'Terrorism' in International Law." *Netherlands International Law Review* 52/1:57-83.

SAUL, BEN. 2006. *Defining Terrorism in International Law*. Oxford: Oxford University Press.

SCHACHTER, OSCAR. 1984. "The Right of States to Use Armed Force." *Michigan Law Review* 82/5-6: 1620-1646.

SCHÄUBLE, WOLFGANG. 2007. Panel on Civil Liberties in an Age of Terror during the "Brussels Forum" on April 27, 2007. Transcript and Video of the Panel retrieved May 13, 2007 (http://www.gmfus.org/brusselsforum/template/agenda_detail.cfm?agenda_id=33).

SCHARF, MICHAEL P. 2004. "Defining Terrorism as the Peacetime Equivalent of War Crimes: Problems and Prospects." *Case Western Reserve Journal of International Law* 36/2-3:359-374.

SCHLAMP, HANS-JÜRGEN. 2007. "Geheimtreffen im Glaspalast." *Der Spiegel* 23/2007: 124-125.

SCHMALENBACH, KIRSTEN. 2006. "Normentheorie vs. Terrorismus: Der Vorrang des UN-Rechts vor EU-Recht." *Juristenzeitung* 61/7: 349-353.

SCHMID, ALEX. 2004. "Terrorism: the Definitional Problem." *Case Western Reserve Journal of International Law* 36/2-3: 375-419.

SCHOLZ, MICHAEL. 2006. *Staatliches Selbstverteidigungsrecht gegen terroristische Gewalt.* Berlin: Duncker & Humblot.

SEIBERT-FOHR, ANJA. 2004. "The Relevance of International Human Rights Standards for Prosecuting Terrorists." Pp. 125-169 in *Terrorism as a Challenge for National and International Law Security versus Liberty?* Edited by Volker Röben, Frank Schorkopf, Silja Vöneky and Christian Walter. Berlin et al: Springer Verlag.

SHAW, MALCOLM N. 2003. *International Law.* New York: Cambridge University Press.

SIMMA, BRUNO. 2003. "Terrorismusbekämpfung und Völkerrecht." Pp. 93-108 in *Neue Bedrohung Terrorismus. Der 11. September und die Folgen.* Edited by Ellen Bos and Antje Helmerich. Münster: Lit Verlag.

SOREL, JEAN MARC. 2003. „Some Questions About the Definition of Terrorism and the Fight Against Its Financing." *European Journal of International Law* 14/2: 365-378.

STATEWATCH. 2001. "Critique of the Council's agreed text on the definition of terrorism." Retrieved June 8, 2007 (http://www.statewatch.org/news/2002/feb/06Aep.htm).

STATEWATCH. 2002. "Decision of the Case *Segi and Gestoras pro Amnistía v. Germany and others.*" Retrieved June9, 2007 (http://www.statewatch.org/terrorlists/SEGI_ECHR.pdf).

STATEWATCH. 2007. "Terrorist Lists – monitoring proscription, designation and asset freezing. EU case-law." Retrieved June 10, 2007 (http://www.statewatch.org/terrorlists/listschallenges.html)

STEIN, TORSTEN und CHRISTIAN VON BUTTLAR. 2005. *Völkerrecht.* Köln: Carl Heymanns Verlag.

STEINBARTH, SEBASTIAN. 2006.Individualrechtsschutz gegen Maßnahmen der EG zur Bekämpfung des internationalen Terrorismus. Die Entscheidungen des EuG in den Rs. „Yusuf u.a." sowie „Kadi". *Zeitschrift für europarechtliche Studien: ZEuS* 9: 269-285.

STOLL, PETER-TOBIAS. 2006. "Die zwei Seiten der Sicherheit: Internationale Kooperation zur Bekämpfung des Terrorismus und die Wahrung von Rechtsstaatlichkeit und Menschenrechten." Pp. 114-130 in *Die Zukunft des Völkerrechts in einer globalisierten Welt.* Edited by Heinrich Böll Stiftung. Baden-Baden: Nomos Verlagsgesellschaft.

TAUS, WOLFGANG. 2006. "Die Bereitschaft zur Tat. Terrorismus am Beispiel von RAF und Al Qaida." *Österreichische militärische Zeitschrift (OeMZ)* 44/6: 699-708.

TOMUSCHAT, CHRISTIAN. 2002. "Der 11. September und seine rechtlichen Konsequenzen." *Europäische Grundrechte-Zeitschrift* 28/21-23: 535-545.

TOMUSCHAT, CHRISTIAN. 2003a. *Human Rights. Between Idealism and Realism.* New York: Oxford University Press.

TOMUSCHAT, CHRISTIAN. 2003b. "The Universal Declaration of Human Rights and the Place of the Charter in Europe: Common Values." Pp. 319-344 in *Praxishandbuch UNO: Die Vereinten Nationen im Lichte globaler Herausforderungen.* Edited by Sabine Schorlemer. Berlin: Springer.

TOMUSCHAT, CHRISTIAN. 2004. "Präventivkrieg zur Bekämpfung des internationalen Terrorismus?" Pp. 121-130 in *Jahrbuch Menschenrechte 2004.* Edited by Deutsches Institut für Menschenrechte and Gabriele von Arnim, Volkmar Deile, Franz-Josef Hutter, Sabine Kurtenbach and Carsten Tessmer. Frankfurt am Main: Suhrkamp.

TOMUSCHAT, CHRISTIAN. 2005. "Further Steps of the Council of Europe with view to Combating Terrorism." *Human Rights Law Journal* 26/5-8: 157-160.

TREATY OF AMSTERDAM AMENDING THE TREATY ON EUROPEAN UNION, THE TREATIES ESTABLISHING THE EUROPEAN COMMUNITIES AND RELATED ACTS. 1997. Amsterdam, 10 November 1997. Retrieved May 13, 2007 (http://europa.eu.int/eur-lex/en/treaties/dat/amsterdam.html#0001010001).

TREATY ON EUROPEAN UNION (TEU). Treaty of Maastricht. 1992. Maastricht, 7 February 1992. Retrieved May 13, 2007 (http://www.eurotreaties.com/maastrichteu.pdf).

UNC. "Charter of the United Nations."
Retrieved April 25, 2007 (http://www.un.org/aboutun/charter/).

UNITED NATIONS. 1948. "Universal Declaration of Human Rights." Adopted and proclaimed by General Assembly resolution 217 A (III) of 10 December 1948. Retrieved May 29, 2007 (http://www.un.org/Overview/rights.html).

UNITED NATIONS. 1966a. "International Covenant on Civil and Political Rights." New York, 16 December 1966. Retrieved May 29, 2007 (http://www.hrweb.org/legal/cpr.html).

UNITED NATIONS. 1966b. "International Covenant on Economic, Social and Cultural Rights." New York, 16 December 1966. Retrieved May 29, 2007 (http://www.hrweb.org/legal/escr.html).

UNITED NATIONS .1967a. Security Council Resolution S/RES/233(1967). "The situation in the Middle East." Retrieved April 30, 2007 (http://daccessdds.un.org/doc/RESOLUTION/GEN/NR0/240/85/IMG/NR024085.pdf?OpenElement).

UNITED NATIONS. 1967b. Security Council Resolution S/RES/234(1967). "The situation in the Middle East." Retrieved April 30, 2007 (http://daccessdds.un.org/doc/RESOLUTION/GEN/NR0/240/85/IMG/NR024085.pdf?OpenElement).

UNITED NATIONS. 1967c. Security Council Resolution S/RES/235(1967). "The situation in the Middle East." Retrieved April 30, 2007 (http://daccessdds.un.org/doc/RESOLUTION/GEN/NR0/240/85/IMG/NR024085.pdf?OpenElement).

UNITED NATIONS. 1967d. Security Council Resolution S/RES/236(1967). "The situation in the Middle East." Retrieved April 30, 2007 (http://daccessdds.un.org/doc/RESOLUTION/GEN/NR0/240/88/IMG/NR024088.pdf?OpenElement).

UNITED NATIONS. 1967e. Security Council Resolution S/RES/237(1967). "The situation in the Middle East." Retrieved April 30, 2007 (http://daccessdds.un.org/doc/RESOLUTION/GEN/NR0/240/89/IMG/NR024089.pdf?OpenElement).

UNITED NATIONS 1974. General Assembly Resolution (XXIX) "Definition of Aggression" 14 December 1974. Retrieved May 4, 2007. (http://daccessdds.un.org/doc/RESOLUTION/GEN/NR0/739/16/IMG/NR073916.pdf?OpenElement).

UNITED NATIONS. 1981. Security Council Resolution S/RES/487(1981). "Iraq-Israel." Retrieved May 3, 2007 (http://daccessdds.un.org/doc/RESOLUTION/GEN/NR0/418/74/IMG/NR041874.pdf?OpenElement).

UNITED NATIONS. 1987. General Assembly Resolution A/RES/42/159. 7 December 1987. "Measures to prevent international terrorism which endangers or takes innocent human lives or jeopardizes fundamental freedoms, and study of the underlying causes of those forms of terrorism and acts of violence which lie in misery, frustration, grievance and despair, and which cause some people to sacrifice human lives, including their own, in an attempt to effect radical changes." Retrieved April 6, 2007 (http://www.un.org/documents/ga/res/42/a42r159.htm).

UNITED NATIONS. 1994. General Assembly Resolution A/RES/49/60. 9 December 1994. "Measures to Eliminate International Terrorism." Retrieved April 6, 2007 (http://www.un.org/documents/ga/res/49/a49r060.htm).

UNITED NATIONS. 1996. General Assembly Resolution A/RES/51/210. 17 December 1996. "Measures to Eliminate International Terrorism." Retrieved April 6, 2007 (http://www.un.org/documents/ga/res/51/a51r210.htm).

UNITED NATIONS. 1998a. Security Council Resolution S/RES/1214(1998). "On the situation in Afghanistan." Retrieved May 2, 2007 (http://daccessdds.un.org/doc/UNDOC/GEN/N98/387/81/PDF/N9838781.pdf?OpenElement).

UNITED NATIONS. 1998b."International Convention for the Suppression of Terrorist Bombings." Signed at New York on 12 January 1998. Retrieved April 6, 2007 (http://www.unodc.org/unodc/terrorism_convention_terrorist_bombing.html)

UNITED NATIONS. 1999. Security Council Resolution S/RES/1267(1999). "On the situation in Afghanistan." Retrieved May 2, 2007 (http://daccessdds.un.org/doc/UNDOC/GEN/N99/300/44/PDF/N9930044.pdf?OpenElement).

UNITED NATIONS. 2000. Security Council Resolution S/RES/1333(2000). "On the Situation in Afghanistan." Retrieved May 2, 2007 (http://daccessdds.un.org/doc/UNDOC/GEN/N00/806/62/PDF/N0080662.pdf?OpenElement).

UNITED NATIONS. 2001a. Security Council Resolution S/RES/1368(2001). "Threats to international peace and security caused by terrorist acts." Retrieved April 6, 2007 (http://daccessdds.un.org/doc/UNDOC/GEN/N01/533/82/PDF/N0153382.pdf?OpenElement).

UNITED NATIONS. 2001b. Security Council Resolution S/RES/1373(2001). "Threats to international peace and security caused by terrorist acts." Retrieved April 6, 2007 (http://daccessdds.un.org/doc/UNDOC/GEN/N01/557/43/PDF/N0155743.pdf?OpenElement).

UNITED NATIONS. 2003. Security Council Resolution S/RES/1456(2003). "High Level Meeting of the Security Council: Combating Terrorism." Retrieved June 10, 2007 (http://daccessdds.un.org/doc/UNDOC/GEN/N03/216/05/PDF/N0321605.pdf?OpenElement).

UNITED NATIONS. 2004a. Security Council Resolution S/RES/1566(2004). "Threats to international peace and security caused by terrorist acts." Retrieved April 6, 2007 (http://daccessdds.un.org/doc/UNDOC/GEN/N04/542/82/PDF/N0454282.pdf?OpenElement).

UNITED NATIONS. 2004b. "A more secure world: Our shared responsibility." Report of the Secretary General's High-Level Panel on Threats, Challenges and Change. Retrieved April 6, 2007 (http://www.un.org/secureworld/report2.pdf).

UNITED NATIONS. 2007a. "Ad Hoc Committee established by General Assembly Resolution 51/210 of 17 December 1996." Status as of 27 March 2007. Retrieved April 6, 2007 (http://www.un.org/law/terrorism/index.html).

UNITED NATIONS. 2007b. "The List of Individuals belonging to or associated with the Taliban; the list of entities belonging to or associated with the Taliban; the List of Individuals belonging to or associated with Al Qaida organization; the List of entities belonging to or associated with Al Qaida organization and individuals and entities that have been removed from the list pursuant to a decision by the 1267 Committee." Last Update 8 June 2007. Retrieved July 1, 2007 (http://www.un.org/sc/committees/1267/consoltablelist.shtml).

VENNEMANN, NICOLA. 2004. "Country Report on the European Union." Pp. 217-266 in *Terrorism as a Challenge for National and International Law Security versus Liberty?* Edited by Volker Röben, Frank Schorkopf, Silja Vöneky and Christian Walter. Berlin et al: Springer Verlag.

VIENNA CONVENTION ON THE LAW OF TREATIES. 1969. Done at Vienna on 23 May 1969. Entered into force on 27 January 1980. Retrieved May 3, 2007 (http://untreaty.un.org/ilc/texts/instruments/english/conventions/1_1_1969.pdf).

VON SCHORLEMER, SABINE. 2003. "Human Rights: Substantive and Institutional Implications of the War Against Terrorism." *European Journal of International Law* 14/2: 265-282.

WANDSCHER, CHRISTIANE. 2006. *Internationaler Terrorismus und Selbstverteidigungsrecht.* Berlin: Duncker & Humblot.

WILSON, RICHARD A. (ed.) 2005. *Human Rights in the 'War on Terror'.* New York: Cambridge University Press.

WOIT, ERNST. 2004. "'Terrorismus'. Problematik und Konsequenzen der Definition." Pp. 143-155 in *Streitkräfte gegen Terroristen. Internationale Militär- und Sicherheitspolitik nach dem 11. September 2001.* Edited by Lothar Schröter. Schkeuditz: Schkeuditzer Buchverlag.

ZEIDAN, SAMI. 2004. "Desperately Seeking Definition: The International Community's Quest for Identifying the Specter of Terrorism." *Cornell International Law Journal* 36/3:491-496.

Appendix

I. United Nations Conventions on Terrorism

1. 'Convention on Offences and Certain Other Acts Committed on Board Aircraft' (1963)
2. 'Convention for the Suppression of Unlawful Seizure of Aircraft' (1970)
   'Convention for the Suppression of Unlawful Acts Against the Safety of Civil Aviation' (1971)
3. 'Protocol for the Suppression of Unlawful Acts of Violence at Airports Serving International Civil Aviation' (1988) Supplementary to the Convention for the Suppression of Unlawful Acts against the Safety of Civil Aviation.
4. 'Convention on the Prevention and Punishment of Crimes Against Internationally Protected Persons' (1973)
5. 'International Convention Against the Taking of Hostages' (1979)
6. 'Convention on the Physical Protection of Nuclear Material' (1980)
7. 'Convention for the Suppression of Unlawful Acts Against the Safety of Maritime Navigation' (1988)
8. 'Protocol for the Suppression of Unlawful Acts Against the Safety of Fixed Platforms Located on the Continental Shelf' (1988)
9. 'Convention on the Marking of Plastic Explosives for the Purpose of Identification' (1991)
10. 'International Convention for the Suppression of Terrorist Bombings' (1998)
11. 'International Convention for the Suppression of the Financing of Terrorism' (1999)
13. 'International Convention for the Suppression of Acts of Nuclear Terrorism' (2005)

The first twelve Conventions are available on the Website of the UN Office of Drugs and Crime: (http://www.unodc.org/unodc/terrorism_conventions.html), retrieved June 12, 2007. The latest Convention, on the Suppression of Acts of Nuclear Terrorism is available at the website of the UN Treaty Collections: (http://untreaty.un.org/English/Terrorism.asp), retrieved June 12, 2007.

II. Framework Decision on Combating Terrorism

Council Framework Decision

of 13 June 2002

on combating terrorism

(2002/475/JHA)

THE COUNCIL OF THE EUROPEAN UNION,

Having regard to the Treaty establishing the European Union, and in particular Article 29, Article 31(e) and Article 34(2)(b) thereof,

Having regard to the proposal from the Commission(1),

Having regard to the opinion of the European Parliament(2),

Whereas:

(1) The European Union is founded on the universal values of human dignity, liberty, equality and solidarity, respect for human rights and fundamental freedoms. It is based on the principle of democracy and the principle of the rule of law, principles which are common to the Member States.

(2) Terrorism constitutes one of the most serious violations of those principles. The La Gomera Declaration adopted at the informal Council meeting on 14 October 1995 affirmed that terrorism constitutes a threat to democracy, to the free exercise of human rights and to economic and social development.

(3) All or some Member States are party to a number of conventions relating to terrorism. The Council of Europe Convention of 27 January 1977 on the Suppression of Terrorism does not regard terrorist offences as political offences or as offences connected with political offences or as offences inspired by political motives. The United Nations has adopted the Convention for the suppression of terrorist bombings of 15 December 1997 and the Convention for the suppression of financing terrorism of 9 December 1999. A draft global Convention against terrorism is currently being negotiated within the United Nations.

(4) At European Union level, on 3 December 1998 the Council adopted the Action Plan of the Council and the Commission on how best to implement the provisions of the Treaty of Amsterdam on an area of freedom, security and justice(3). Account should also be taken of the Council Conclusions of 20 September 2001 and of the Extraordinary European Council plan of action to combat terrorism of 21 September 2001. Terrorism was referred to in the conclusions of the Tampere European Council of 15 and 16 October 1999, and of the Santa María da Feira European Council of 19

and 20 June 2000. It was also mentioned in the Commission communication to the Council and the European Parliament on the biannual update of the scoreboard to review progress on the creation of an area of "freedom, security and justice" in the European Union (second half of 2000). Furthermore, on 5 September 2001 the European Parliament adopted a recommendation on the role of the European Union in combating terrorism. It should, moreover, be recalled that on 30 July 1996 twenty-five measures to fight against terrorism were advocated by the leading industrialised countries (G7) and Russia meeting in Paris.

(5) The European Union has adopted numerous specific measures having an impact on terrorism and organised crime, such as the Council Decision of 3 December 1998 instructing Europol to deal with crimes committed or likely to be committed in the course of terrorist activities against life, limb, personal freedom or property(4); Council Joint Action 96/610/JHA of 15 October 1996 concerning the creation and maintenance of a Directory of specialised counter-terrorist competences, skills and expertise to facilitate counter-terrorism cooperation between the Member States of the European Union(5); Council Joint Action 98/428/JHA of 29 June 1998 on the creation of a European Judicial Network(6), with responsibilities in terrorist offences, in particular Article 2; Council Joint Action 98/733/JHA of 21 December 1998 on making it a criminal offence to participate in a criminal organisation in the Member States of the European Union(7); and the Council Recommendation of 9 December 1999 on cooperation in combating the financing of terrorist groups(8).

(6) The definition of terrorist offences should be approximated in all Member States, including those offences relating to terrorist groups. Furthermore, penalties and sanctions should be provided for natural and legal persons having committed or being liable for such offences, which reflect the seriousness of such offences.

(7) Jurisdictional rules should be established to ensure that the terrorist offence may be effectively prosecuted.

(8) Victims of terrorist offences are vulnerable, and therefore specific measures are necessary with regard to them.

(9) Given that the objectives of the proposed action cannot be sufficiently achieved by the Member States unilaterally, and can therefore, because of the need for reciprocity, be better achieved at the level of the Union, the Union may adopt measures, in accordance with the principle of subsidiarity. In accordance with the principle of proportionality, this Framework Decision does not go beyond what is necessary in order to achieve those objectives.

(10) This Framework Decision respects fundamental rights as guaranteed by the European Convention for the Protection of Human Rights and Fundamental Freedoms and as they emerge from the constitutional traditions common to the Member States as principles of Community law. The Union observes the principles recognised by Article 6(2) of the Treaty on European Union and reflected in the

Charter of Fundamental Rights of the European Union, notably Chapter VI thereof. Nothing in this Framework Decision may be interpreted as being intended to reduce or restrict fundamental rights or freedoms such as the right to strike, freedom of assembly, of association or of expression, including the right of everyone to form and to join trade unions with others for the protection of his or her interests and the related right to demonstrate.

(11) Actions by armed forces during periods of armed conflict, which are governed by international humanitarian law within the meaning of these terms under that law, and, inasmuch as they are governed by other rules of international law, actions by the armed forces of a State in the exercise of their official duties are not governed by this Framework Decision,

HAS ADOPTED THIS FRAMEWORK DECISION:

Article 1 Terrorist offences and fundamental rights and principles

1. Each Member State shall take the necessary measures to ensure that the intentional acts referred to below in points (a) to (i), as defined as offences under national law, which, given their nature or context, may seriously damage a country or an international organisation where committed with the aim of:

- seriously intimidating a population, or
- unduly compelling a Government or international organisation to perform or abstain from performing any act, or
- seriously destabilising or destroying the fundamental political, constitutional, economic or social structures of a country or an international organisation,

shall be deemed to be terrorist offences:

(a) attacks upon a person's life which may cause death;

(b) attacks upon the physical integrity of a person;

(c) kidnapping or hostage taking;

(d) causing extensive destruction to a Government or public facility, a transport system, an infrastructure facility, including an information system, a fixed platform located on the continental shelf, a public place or private property likely to endanger human life or result in major economic loss;

(e) seizure of aircraft, ships or other means of public or goods transport;

(f) manufacture, possession, acquisition, transport, supply or use of weapons, explosives or of nuclear, biological or chemical weapons, as well as research into, and development of, biological and chemical weapons;

(g) release of dangerous substances, or causing fires, floods or explosions the effect of which is to endanger human life;

(h) interfering with or disrupting the supply of water, power or any other fundamental natural resource the effect of which is to endanger human life;

(i) threatening to commit any of the acts listed in (a) to (h).

2. This Framework Decision shall not have the effect of altering the obligation to respect fundamental rights and fundamental legal principles as enshrined in Article 6 of the Treaty on European Union.

Article 2 Offences relating to a terrorist group

1. For the purposes of this Framework Decision, "terrorist group" shall mean: a structured group of more than two persons, established over a period of time and acting in concert to commit terrorist offences. "Structured group" shall mean a group that is not randomly formed for the immediate commission of an offence and that does not need to have formally defined roles for its members, continuity of its membership or a developed structure.

2. Each Member State shall take the necessary measures to ensure that the following intentional acts are punishable:

(a) directing a terrorist group;

(b) participating in the activities of a terrorist group, including by supplying information or material resources, or by funding its activities in any way, with knowledge of the fact that such participation will contribute to the criminal activities of the terrorist group.

Article 3 Offences linked to terrorist activities

Each Member State shall take the necessary measures to ensure that terrorist-linked offences include the following acts:

(a) aggravated theft with a view to committing one of the acts listed in Article 1(1);

(b) extortion with a view to the perpetration of one of the acts listed in Article 1(1);

(c) drawing up false administrative documents with a view to committing one of the acts listed in Article 1(1)(a) to (h) and Article 2(2)(b).

Article 4 Inciting, aiding or abetting, and attempting

1. Each Member State shall take the necessary measures to ensure that inciting or aiding or abetting an offence referred to in Article 1(1), Articles 2 or 3 is made punishable.

2. Each Member State shall take the necessary measures to ensure that attempting to commit an offence referred to in Article 1(1) and Article 3, with the exception of possession as provided for in Article 1(1)(f) and the offence referred to in Article 1(1)(i), is made punishable.

Article 5 Penalties

1. Each Member State shall take the necessary measures to ensure that the offences referred to in Articles 1 to 4 are punishable by effective, proportionate and dissuasive criminal penalties, which may entail extradition.

2. Each Member State shall take the necessary measures to ensure that the terrorist offences referred to in Article 1(1) and offences referred to in Article 4, inasmuch as they relate to terrorist offences, are punishable by custodial sentences heavier than those imposable under national law for such offences in the absence of the special intent required pursuant to Article 1(1), save where the sentences imposable are already the maximum possible sentences under national law.

3. Each Member State shall take the necessary measures to ensure that offences listed in Article 2 are punishable by custodial sentences, with a maximum sentence of not less than fifteen years for the offence referred to in Article 2(2)(a), and for the offences listed in Article 2(2)(b) a maximum sentence of not less than eight years. In so far as the offence referred to in Article 2(2)(a) refers only to the act in Article 1(1)(i), the maximum sentence shall not be less than eight years.

Article 6 Particular circumstances

Each Member State may take the necessary measures to ensure that the penalties referred to in Article 5 may be reduced if the offender:

(a) renounces terrorist activity, and

(b) provides the administrative or judicial authorities with information which they would not otherwise have been able to obtain, helping them to:

(i) prevent or mitigate the effects of the offence;

(ii) identify or bring to justice the other offenders;

(iii) find evidence; or

(iv) prevent further offences referred to in Articles 1 to 4.

Article 7 Liability of legal persons

1. Each Member State shall take the necessary measures to ensure that legal persons can be held liable for any of the offences referred to in Articles 1 to 4 committed for their benefit by any person, acting either individually or as part of an organ of the legal person, who has a leading position within the legal person, based on one of the following:

(a) a power of representation of the legal person;

(b) an authority to take decisions on behalf of the legal person;

(c) an authority to exercise control within the legal person.

2. Apart from the cases provided for in paragraph 1, each Member State shall take the necessary measures to ensure that legal persons can be held liable where the lack of supervision or control by a person referred to in paragraph 1 has made possible the commission of any of the offences referred to in Articles 1 to 4 for the benefit of that legal person by a person under its authority.

3. Liability of legal persons under paragraphs 1 and 2 shall not exclude criminal proceedings against natural persons who are perpetrators, instigators or accessories in any of the offences referred to in Articles 1 to 4.

Article 8 Penalties for legal persons

Each Member State shall take the necessary measures to ensure that a legal person held liable pursuant to Article 7 is punishable by effective, proportionate and dissuasive penalties, which shall include criminal or non-criminal fines and may include other penalties, such as:

(a) exclusion from entitlement to public benefits or aid;

(b) temporary or permanent disqualification from the practice of commercial activities;

(c) placing under judicial supervision;

(d) a judicial winding-up order;

(e) temporary or permanent closure of establishments which have been used for committing the offence.

Article 9 Jurisdiction and prosecution

1. Each Member State shall take the necessary measures to establish its jurisdiction over the offences referred to in Articles 1 to 4 where:

(a) the offence is committed in whole or in part in its territory. Each Member State may extend its jurisdiction if the offence is committed in the territory of a Member State;

(b) the offence is committed on board a vessel flying its flag or an aircraft registered there;

(c) the offender is one of its nationals or residents;

(d) the offence is committed for the benefit of a legal person established in its territory;

(e) the offence is committed against the institutions or people of the Member State in question or against an institution of the European Union or a body set up in accordance with the Treaty establishing the European Community or the Treaty on European Union and based in that Member State.

2. When an offence falls within the jurisdiction of more than one Member State and when any of the States concerned can validly prosecute on the basis of the same facts, the Member States concerned shall cooperate in order to decide which of them will prosecute the offenders with the aim, if possible, of centralising proceedings in a single Member State. To this end, the Member States may have recourse to any body or mechanism established within the European Union in order to facilitate cooperation between their judicial authorities and the coordination of their action. Sequential account shall be taken of the following factors:

- the Member State shall be that in the territory of which the acts were committed,

- the Member State shall be that of which the perpetrator is a national or resident,

- the Member State shall be the Member State of origin of the victims,

- the Member State shall be that in the territory of which the perpetrator was found.

3. Each Member State shall take the necessary measures also to establish its jurisdiction over the offences referred to in Articles 1 to 4 in cases where it refuses to hand over or extradite a person suspected or convicted of such an offence to another Member State or to a third country.

4. Each Member State shall ensure that its jurisdiction covers cases in which any of the offences referred to in Articles 2 and 4 has been committed in whole or in part within its territory, wherever the terrorist group is based or pursues its criminal activities.

5. This Article shall not exclude the exercise of jurisdiction in criminal matters as laid down by a Member State in accordance with its national legislation.

Article 10 Protection of, and assistance to, victims

1. Member States shall ensure that investigations into, or prosecution of, offences covered by this Framework Decision are not dependent on a report or accusation made by a person subjected to the offence, at least if the acts were committed on the territory of the Member State.

2. In addition to the measures laid down in the Council Framework Decision 2001/220/JHA of 15 March 2001 on the standing of victims in criminal proceedings(9), each Member State shall, if necessary, take all measures possible to ensure appropriate assistance for victims' families.

Article 11 Implementation and reports

1. Member States shall take the necessary measures to comply with this Framework Decision by 31 December 2002.

2. By 31 December 2002, Member States shall forward to the General Secretariat of the Council and to the Commission the text of the provisions transposing into their national law the obligations imposed on them under this Framework Decision. On the basis of a report drawn up from that information and a report from the Commission, the Council shall assess, by 31 December 2003, whether Member States have taken the necessary measures to comply with this Framework Decision.

3. The Commission report shall specify, in particular, transposition into the criminal law of the Member States of the obligation referred to in Article 5(2).

Article 12 Territorial application

This Framework Decision shall apply to Gibraltar.

Article 13 Entry into force

This Framework Decision shall enter into force on the day of its publication in the Official Journal.

Done at Luxembourg, 13 June 2002.

For the Council

The President

M. Rajoy Brey

(1) OJ C 332 E, 27.11.2001, p. 300.

(2) Opinion delivered on 6 February 2002 (not yet published in the Official Journal).

(3) OJ C 19, 23.1.1999, p. 1.

(4) OJ C 26, 30.1.1999, p. 22.

(5) OJ L 273, 25.10.1996, p. 1.

(6) OJ L 191, 7.7.1998, p. 4.

(7) OJ L 351, 29.12.1998, p. 1.

(8) OJ C 373, 23.12.1999, p. 1.

(9) OJ L 82, 22.3.2001, p. 1.

(Only European Community legislation printed in the paper edition of the *Official Journal of the European Union* is deemed authentic.)

III. European Convention for the Protection of Human Rights and Fundamental Freedoms

Articles 1-18 (excluding Section II on the European Court of Human Rights)

and Protocol 13

Article 1 Obligation to respect human rights

The High Contracting Parties shall secure to everyone within their jurisdiction the rights and freedoms defined in Section I of this Convention.

SECTION I RIGHTS AND FREEDOMS

Article 2 Right to life

1. Everyone's right to life shall be protected by law. No one shall be deprived of his life intentionally save in the execution of a sentence of a court following his conviction of a crime for which this penalty is provided by law.
2. Deprivation of life shall not be regarded as inflicted in contravention of this article when it results from the use of force which is no more than absolutely necessary:

a in defence of any person from unlawful violence;

b in order to effect a lawful arrest or to prevent the escape of a person lawfully detained;

c in action lawfully taken for the purpose of quelling a riot or insurrection.

Article 3 Prohibition of torture

No one shall be subjected to torture or to inhuman or degrading treatment or punishment.

Article 4 Prohibition of slavery and forced labour

1. No one shall be held in slavery or servitude.
2. No one shall be required to perform forced or compulsory labour.
3. For the purpose of this article the term —forced or compulsory labour shall not include:

a any work required to be done in the ordinary course of detention imposed according to the provisions of Article 5 of this Convention or during conditional release from such detention;

b any service of a military character or, in case of conscientious objectors in countries where they are recognised, service exacted instead of compulsory military service;

c any service exacted in case of an emergency or calamity threatening the life or well-being of the community;
d any work or service which forms part of normal civic obligations.

Article 5 Right to liberty and security

1. Everyone has the right to liberty and security of person. No one shall be deprived of his liberty save in the following cases and in accordance with a procedure prescribed by law:
a the lawful detention of a person after conviction by a competent court;
b the lawful arrest or detention of a person for non-compliance with the lawful order of a court or in order to secure the fulfilment of any obligation prescribed by law;
c the lawful arrest or detention of a person effected for the purpose of bringing him before the competent legal authority on reasonable suspicion of having committed an offence or when it is reasonably considered necessary to prevent his committing an offence or fleeing after having done so;
d the detention of a minor by lawful order for the purpose of educational supervision or his lawful detention for the purpose of bringing him before the competent legal authority;
e the lawful detention of persons for the prevention of the spreading of infectious diseases, of persons of unsound mind, alcoholics or drug addicts or vagrants;
f the lawful arrest or detention of a person to prevent his effecting an unauthorised entry into the country or of a person against whom action is being taken with a view to deportation or extradition.
2. Everyone who is arrested shall be informed promptly, in a language which he understands, of the reasons for his arrest and of any charge against him.
3. Everyone arrested or detained in accordance with the provisions of paragraph 1.c of this article shall be brought promptly before a judge or other officer authorised by law to exercise judicial power and shall be entitled to trial within a reasonable time or to release pending trial. Release may be conditioned by guarantees to appear for trial.
4. Everyone who is deprived of his liberty by arrest or detention shall be entitled to take proceedings by which the lawfulness of his detention shall be decided speedily by a court and his release ordered if the detention is not lawful.
5. Everyone who has been the victim of arrest or detention in contravention of the provisions of this article shall have an enforceable right to compensation.

Article 6 Right to a fair trial

1. In the determination of his civil rights and obligations or of any criminal charge against him, everyone is entitled to a fair and public hearing within a reasonable time by an independent and impartial tribunal established by law. Judgment shall be pronounced publicly but the press and public may be excluded from all or part of the trial in the interests of morals, public order or national security in a democratic society, where the interests of juveniles or the protection of the private life of the

parties so require, or to the extent strictly necessary in the opinion of the court in special circumstances where publicity would prejudice the interests of justice.

2. Everyone charged with a criminal offence shall be presumed innocent until proved guilty according to law.

3. Everyone charged with a criminal offence has the following minimum rights:

a to be informed promptly, in a language which he understands and in detail, of the nature and cause of the accusation against him;

b to have adequate time and facilities for the preparation of his defence;

c to defend himself in person or through legal assistance of his own choosing or, if he has not sufficient means to pay for legal assistance, to be given it free when the interests of justice so require;

d to examine or have examined witnesses against him and to obtain the attendance and examination of witnesses on his behalf under the same conditions as witnesses against him;

e to have the free assistance of an interpreter if he cannot understand or speak the language used in court.

Article 7 No punishment without law

1. No one shall be held guilty of any criminal offence on account of any act or omission which did not constitute a criminal offence under national or international law at the time when it was committed. Nor shall a heavier penalty be imposed than the one that was applicable at the time the criminal offence was committed.

2. This article shall not prejudice the trial and punishment of any person for any act or omission which, at the time when it was committed, was criminal according to the general principles of law recognised by civilised nations.

Article 8 Right to respect for private and family life

1. Everyone has the right to respect for his private and family life, his home and his correspondence.

2. There shall be no interference by a public authority with the exercise of this right except such as is in accordance with the law and is necessary in a democratic society in the interests of national security, public safety or the economic well-being of the country, for the prevention of disorder or crime, for the protection of health or morals, or for the protection of the rights and freedoms of others.

Article 9 Freedom of thought, conscience and religion

1. Everyone has the right to freedom of thought, conscience and religion; this right includes freedom to change his religion or belief and freedom, either alone or in community with others and in public or private, to manifest his religion or belief, in worship, teaching, practice and observance.

2. Freedom to manifest one's religion or beliefs shall be subject only to such limitations as are prescribed by law and are necessary in a democratic society in the interests of public safety, for the protection of public order, health or morals, or for the protection of the rights and freedoms of others.

Article 10 Freedom of expression

1. Everyone has the right to freedom of expression. This right shall include freedom to hold opinions and to receive and impart information and ideas without interference by public authority and regardless of frontiers. This article shall not prevent States from requiring the licensing of broadcasting, television or cinema enterprises.
2. The exercise of these freedoms, since it carries with it duties and responsibilities, may be subject to such formalities, conditions, restrictions or penalties as are prescribed by law and are necessary in a democratic society, in the interests of national security, territorial integrity or public safety, for the prevention of disorder or crime, for the protection of health or morals, for the protection of the reputation or rights of others, for preventing the disclosure of information received in confidence, or for maintaining the authority and impartiality of the judiciary.

Article 11 Freedom of assembly and association

1. Everyone has the right to freedom of peaceful assembly and to freedom of association with others, including the right to form and to join trade unions for the protection of his interests.
2. No restrictions shall be placed on the exercise of these rights other than such as are prescribed by law and are necessary in a democratic society in the interests of national security or public safety, for the prevention of disorder or crime, for the protection of health or morals or for the protection of the rights and freedoms of others. This article shall not prevent the imposition of lawful restrictions on the exercise of these rights by members of the armed forces, of the police or of the administration of the State.

Article 12 Right to marry

Men and women of marriageable age have the right to marry and to found a family, according to the national laws governing the exercise of this right.

Article 13 Right to an effective remedy

Everyone whose rights and freedoms as set forth in this Convention are violated shall have an effective remedy before a national authority notwithstanding that the violation has been committed by persons acting in an official capacity.

Article 14 Prohibition of discrimination

The enjoyment of the rights and freedoms set forth in this Convention shall be secured without discrimination on any ground such as sex, race, colour, language, religion, political or other opinion, national or social origin, association with a national minority, property, birth or other status.

Article 15 Derogation in time of emergency

1. In time of war or other public emergency threatening the life of the nation any High Contracting Party may take measures derogating from its obligations under this Convention to the extent strictly required by the exigencies of the situation, provided that such measures are not inconsistent with its other obligations under international law.
2. No derogation from Article 2, except in respect of deaths resulting from lawful acts of war, or from Articles 3, 4 (paragraph 1) and 7 shall be made under this provision.
3. Any High Contracting Party availing itself of this right of derogation shall keep the Secretary General of the Council of Europe fully informed of the measures which it has taken and the reasons therefor. It shall also inform the Secretary General of the Council of Europe when such measures have ceased to operate and the provisions of the Convention are again being fully executed.

Article 16 Restrictions on political activity of aliens

Nothing in Articles 10, 11 and 14 shall be regarded as preventing the High Contracting Parties from imposing restrictions on the political activity of aliens.

Article 17 Prohibition of abuse of rights

Nothing in this Convention may be interpreted as implying for any State, group or person any right to engage in any activity or perform any act aimed at the destruction of any of the rights and freedoms set forth herein or at their limitation to a greater extent than is provided for in the Convention.

Article 18 Limitation on use of restrictions on rights

The restrictions permitted under this Convention to the said rights and freedoms shall not be applied for any purpose other than those for which they have been prescribed.

1952 Protocol to the ECHR

Protocol to the Convention for the Protection of Human Rights and Fundamental Freedoms: Paris, 20 March 1952.

The governments signatory hereto, being members of the Council of Europe,
Being resolved to take steps to ensure the collective enforcement of certain rights and freedoms other than those already included in Section I of the Convention for the Protection of Human Rights and Fundamental Freedoms signed at Rome on 4 November 1950 (hereinafter referred to as —the Convention"),

Have agreed as follows:

Article 1 Protection of property
Every natural or legal person is entitled to the peaceful enjoyment of his possessions. No one shall be deprived of his possessions except in the public interest and subject to the conditions provided for by law and by the general principles of international law.
The preceding provisions shall not, however, in any way impair the right of a State to enforce such laws as it deems necessary to control the use of property in accordance with the general interest or to secure the payment of taxes or other contributions or penalties.

Article 2 Right to education
No person shall be denied the right to education. In the exercise of any functions which it assumes in relation to education and to teaching, the State shall respect the right of parents to ensure such education and teaching in conformity with their own religious and philosophical convictions.

Article 3 Right to free elections
The High Contracting Parties undertake to hold free elections at reasonable intervals by secret ballot, under conditions which will ensure the free expression of the opinion of the people in the choice of the legislature.

Article 4 Territorial application
Any High Contracting Party may at the time of signature or ratification or at any time thereafter communicate to the Secretary General of the Council of Europe a declaration stating the extent to which it undertakes that the provisions of the present Protocol shall apply to such of the territories for the international relations of which it is responsible as are named therein.

Any High Contracting Party which has communicated a declaration in virtue of the preceding paragraph may from time to time communicate a further declaration modifying the terms of any former declaration or terminating the application of the provisions of this Protocol in respect of any territory.
A declaration made in accordance with this article shall be deemed to have been made in accordance with paragraph 1 of Article 56 of the Convention.

Article 5 Relationship to the Convention
As between the High Contracting Parties the provisions of Articles 1, 2, 3 and 4 of this Protocol shall be regarded as additional articles to the Convention and all the provisions of the Convention shall apply accordingly.

Article 6 Signature and ratification
This Protocol shall be open for signature by the members of the Council of Europe, who are the signatories of the Convention; it shall be ratified at the same time as or after the ratification of the Convention. It shall enter into force after the deposit of ten instruments of ratification. As regards any signatory ratifying subsequently, the Protocol shall enter into force at the date of the deposit of its instrument of ratification.
The instruments of ratification shall be deposited with the Secretary General of the Council of Europe, who will notify all members of the names of those who have ratified.
Done at Paris on the 20th day of March 1952, in English and French, both texts being equally authentic, in a single copy which shall remain deposited in the archives of the Council of Europe. The Secretary General shall transmit certified copies to each of the signatory governments.

Protocol No. 13 to the Convention for the Protection of Human Rights and Fundamental Freedoms Concerning the abolition of the death penalty in all circumstances. Vilnius, 3.V.2002

The member States of the Council of Europe signatory hereto, Convinced that everyone's right to life is a basic value in a democratic society and that the abolition of the death penalty is essential for the protection of this right and for the full recognition of the inherent dignity of all human beings;
Wishing to strengthen the protection of the right to life guaranteed by the Convention for the Protection of Human Rights and Fundamental Freedoms signed at Rome on 4 November 1950 (hereinafter referred to as —the Convention");
Noting that Protocol No. 6 to the Convention, concerning the Abolition of the Death Penalty, signed at Strasbourg on 28 April 1983, does not exclude the death penalty in respect of acts committed in time of war or of imminent threat of war;
Being resolved to take the final step in order to abolish the death penalty in all circumstances,

Have agreed as follows:

Article 1 Abolition of the death penalty
The death penalty shall be abolished. No one shall be condemned to such penalty or executed.

Article 2 Prohibitions of derogations
No derogation from the provisions of this Protocol shall be made under Article 15 of the Convention.

Article 3 Prohibitions of reservations
No reservation may be made under Article 57 of the Convention in respect of the provisions of this Protocol.

Article 4 Territorial application
1. Any state may, at the time of signature or when depositing its instrument of ratification, acceptance or approval, specify the territory or territories to which this Protocol shall apply.
2. Any state may at any later date, by a declaration addressed to the Secretary General of the Council of Europe, extend the application of this Protocol to any other territory specified in the declaration. In respect of such territory the Protocol shall enter into

force on the first day of the month following the expiration of a period of three months after the date of receipt by the Secretary General of such declaration.

3. Any declaration made under the two preceding paragraphs may, in respect of any territory specified in such declaration, be withdrawn or modified by a notification addressed to the Secretary General. The withdrawal or modification shall become effective on the first day of the month following the expiration of a period of three months after the date of receipt of such notification by the Secretary General.

Article 5 Relationship to the Convention

As between the states Parties the provisions of Articles 1 to 4 of this Protocol shall be regarded as additional articles to the Convention, and all the provisions of the Convention shall apply accordingly.

Article 6 Signature and ratification

This Protocol shall be open for signature by member states of the Council of Europe which have signed the Convention. It is subject to ratification, acceptance or approval. A member state of the Council of Europe may not ratify, accept or approve this Protocol without previously or simultaneously ratifying the Convention. Instruments of ratification, acceptance or approval shall be deposited with the Secretary General of the Council of Europe.

Article 7 Entry into force

1. This Protocol shall enter into force on the first day of the month following the expiration of a period of three months after the date on which ten member states of the Council of Europe have expressed their consent to be bound by the Protocol in accordance with the provisions of Article 6.
2. In respect of any member state which subsequently expresses its consent to be bound by it, the Protocol shall enter into force on the first day of the month following the expiration of a period of three months after the date of the deposit of the instrument of ratification, acceptance or approval.

Article 8 Depositary functions

The Secretary General of the Council of Europe shall notify all the member states of the Council of Europe of:

a any signature;

b the deposit of any instrument of ratification, acceptance or approval;

c any date of entry into force of this Protocol in accordance with Articles 4 and 7;

d any other act, notification or communication relating to this Protocol;

In witness whereof the undersigned, being duly authorised thereto, have signed this Protocol. Done at Vilnius, this 3rd day of May 2002, in English and in French, both texts being equally authentic, in a single copy which shall be deposited in the archives of the Council of Europe. The Secretary General of the Council of Europe shall transmit certified copies to each member state of the Council of Europe.

IV. List of Cases Relating to the "Terror Lists" at the European Courts

The European Court of First Instance

Applicant(s)	Date	Case reference	Details	Judgment
Abdirisak Aden and Others [al-Barakaat, Sweden]	10 December 2001	T-306/01	The Applicants argued that the EU Council had exceeded its powers in freezing the resources associates of the Taleban under Regulation 467/2001 (March 2001) under Articles 60 EC and 301 EC. They sought annulment of Regulations 467/2001 and 2199/2001 (implementing legislation), arguing that the "fundamental legal principle of the right to a fair and equitable hearing" had been disregarded. Ultimately, the al-Barakaat trio were removed from the UN and EU lists (see below).	Application for interim relief ("urgency proceedings") dismissed, 7 May 2002 [2002] ECR II-2387 Dismissed, 21 September 2005 (appealed to ECJ, see case C-402/05 P, below)
Yassin Abdullah Kadi [Saudi Arabian businessman]	18 December 2001	T-315/01	Also concerns Regulation 467/2001 (above). Applicant sought an annulment of the Regulation as far as it relates to him, arguing interference with property rights and violation of the Community Law principle of	Dismissed, 21 September 2005

			effective judicial control because of the failure to provide any opportunity for redress. Later removed from ECJ register - applicant presumably delisted	
Omar Mohamed Othman [Jordanian residing in the UK]	17 December 2001	T-318/01	Also seeks annulment of Regulation 467/2001 (above) and implementing Regulation 2062/2001. Argues misuse of Council powers and violation of articles 3 and 8, ECHR and violation of the principle of subsidiarity.	Not yet decided.
Congrès National du Kurdistan [in respect to PKK]	2 July 2002	T-206/02 Note: the UK and the Commission supported the Council	Sought annulment of the decision to proscribe the PKK arguing defamation, erroneous judgment, denial of freedom of expression and sought damages of 10,000 euro. Also argued failure to provide procedural remedies and that the PKK has been advocating non-violence since 1999.	Dismissed, 15. February 2005
Organisation des Modjahedines du Peuple d'Iran (OMPI) [PMOI]	26 July 2002	T-228/02	The Applicants sought partial annulment of the Decisions and Common Positions implementing Common Position 2001/931 and Regulation 2580/2001 (on freezing the assets of "foreign"	Ruling in favour of applicant, 12 December 2006

			terrorists) and damages of 1 euro. In support of their claims, the applicants argued breach of the right to defence, failure to recognise its actions as resistance to occupation and tyranny and breach of the principle of non-discrimination.	
Kurdistan Workers Party (PKK) and Kurdistan National Congress (KNK)	31 July 2002	T-229/02 Note: the UK and the Commission supported the Council	The Applicants sought annulment of the Decision to proscribe them and related damages. They argued that the EU had breached its own procedural rules in failing to recognise that the PKK had renounced violence, breach of civil, cultural and political rights, breach of fundamental rights and principles of Community law and misuse of Council powers.	Dismissed, 15 February 2005 (appealed to ECJ, see case C-229/05 P, below)
Chafiq Ayadi [Irish resident]	22 August 2002	T-253/02	Seeks annulment of Regulation 881/2002 implementing Regulation 467/2001 (on freezing Taleban associates' assets. above). Argues that UN measures do not impose a duty to apply such measures, misuse of Council and Commission powers and violation of the principles of subsidiarity and	Dismissed, 12 July 2005

			proportionality and respect for human rights. Also argues failure to provide opportunity for judicial redress and reasons.	
Gestoras Pro Amnistía association, Juan Mari Olano Olano and Julen Zelarain Errasti [a Basque Group and associated individuals]	31 October 2002	T-333/02	The Applicants sought combined damages of 1.2 million euro. Arguments identical to those in case T-338/02, below.	Dismissed, 7 June 2004 (appealed to ECJ, see case C-354/04 P, below)
SEGI association, Araitz Zubimendi Izaga and Aritza Galarraga [a Basque Group and associated individuals]	13 November 2002	T-338/02	The Applicants sought combined damages of 1.2 million euro. They argued that their fundamental rights to the presumption of innocence, a fair hearing, freedom of speech, self-determination and privacy had been breached. They also argued that the procedure used to adopt Common Position 2001/931 and Regulation 2580/2001 was unlawful and failed to provide them with adequate defence rights.	Dismissed, 7 June 2004 (appealed to ECJ, see case C-355/04 P, below)
Jose Maria Sison [accused of being head of the "New	6 February 2003	T-47/03	Seeks partial annulment of the Decisions to proscribe Mr. Sison, annulment of Regulation 2580/2001 and damages	Application for interim relief dismissed, 15 May 2003

People's Army" in The Philippines, residing in Holland]			of at least 100,000 euro. Argues that Mr. Sison is a political refugee recognised by the Netherlands, that he is not head of the New People's Army, that his fundamental rights under articles 6, 7, 10 and 11 ECHR have been breached. Also argues that Regulation 2580/2001 is unlawful.	[2003] ECR I-2047
Jose Maria Sison	24 March 2003	T-110/03	Mr. Sison's lawyers requested from the General Secretariat of the EU Council all documents which formed the of the Decision to proscribe the applicant and the New People's Army as well as access to any information regarding which Member States provided documents mentioned in the contested Decision. The Council refused on the grounds that these documents constituted "sensitive information" (and exception in the Regulation on public access to documents) and suggested their release would breach the Council's Security Regulations.	Dismissed, 26 April 2005
Jose Maria Sison	30 April 2003	T-150/03	Seeks annulment of Council's Decision to reject Mr. Sision's lawyers' "confirmatory	Dismissed, 26 April 2005

			application" (appeal) contesting the Decision of the Council to refuse access the to documents requested above.	
Stichting al-Aqsa	19 September 2003	T-327/03	The Applicants sought annulment of the Decision to proscribe them and asked the Court to declare inapplicable Regulation 2580/2001 and provide related damages. They argue violation of procedural rules and the right to a fair hearing and breach of other fundamental rights.	Not yet decided.
Jose Maria Sison	12 December 2003	T-405/03	Joined to cases T-110/03 and T-150/03 (above). Concerns reply to "confirmatory application".	Dismissed, 26 April 2005
Faraj Hassan [UK resident]	12 February 2004	T-49/04	Seeks annulment of Regulation 881/2002 implementing Regulation 467/2001 (on freezing Taleban associates' assets. above) as far it relates to the proscription of the applicant, and related damages. Argues that the measures "annihilate his peaceful enjoyment of his property and his private and family life" and that the defendants "wholly failed to provide	Dismissed, 12 July 2006

			him, both before and after the decision was taken, with a fair hearing or effective remedy". Also claims that the measures violate the principle of proportionality.	
Zubeyir Aydar on behalf of Kongra-Gel and 10 others [proscribed as alias of PKK]	25 June 2004	T-253/04	The Applicants seek annulment of the Decision to proscribe them, arguing "failure to apply accessible, objective criteria to the correct facts", breach of freedom of expression, breach of principles of Community law and misuse of power. Also argues failure to ensure right to a fair hearing.	Not yet decided.
Hani El Sayyed Elsebai Yusef [UK resident]	6 January 2006	T-2/06	Seeks annulment of Regulation 881/2002 implementing Regulation 467/2001 (on freezing Taleban associates' assets. above) as far it relates to the proscription of the applicant. The applicant was listed pursuant to Regulation (EC) No 1629/2005 of 5 October 2005, amending for the 54th time Council Regulation (EC) No 881/2002. The Regulation 1629/2005 was published in the Official Journal of the European Union on 6 October 2005 so the	Rejected (application received too late), 31 May 2006

			time-limit for commencing annulment proceedings expired on 30 December 2005.	
Al-Bashir Mohammed Al-Faqih [Libyan, UK resident]	5 May 2006	T-135/06	Seeks the annulment of Regulation 246/2006 by which the applicant was inluded in the list of persons, groups and entities associated with Usama bin Laden, the Al-Qaida network and the Taliban (pursuant to Article 2 of Regulation No 881/2002). Argues that the Council was not competent to adopt Article 2 of Regulation in that Articles 60 EC, 301 EC and 308 EC do not confer on the Council the power to do so. Also argues that the Council and the Commission misused their powers and that Article 2 of Regulation No 881/2002 as amended infringes the fundamental principles of Community law (subsidiarity, proportionality and respect for fundamental rights). Also cites infringement of an essential procedural requirement in the adoption of Regulation No 881/2002 to state adequate reasons why	Not decided yet.

			the measures considered necessary cannot be determined by individual Member States.	
Sanabel Relief Agency Ltd [UK-based]	5 May 2006	T-136/06	Pleas and arguments identical to those in case T-135/06, above	Not decided yet.
Ghunia Abdrabba [UK resident]	5 May 2006	T-137/06	Pleas and arguments identical to those in case T-135/06, above	Not decided yet.
Taher Nasuf [UK resident]	5 May 2006	T-138/06	Pleas and arguments identical to those in case T-135/06, above	Not decided yet.
Mohamed El Morabit (Netherlands)	16 February 2007	T-37/07	Annul EC Regulation No 2580/2001	Not decided yet.
Ahmed Hamdi (Netherlands)	12 March 2007	T-75/07	Common Position 2002/402/CFSP wrongly used as basis for Regulation 2580/2001/EC. The latter regulation should therefore not be applied for the applicant. Decision 2006/1008/EC should be annulled, the Council should pay the costs.	Not decided yet.
People's Mojahedin Organization of Iran (France)	9 May 2007	T-157/07	Annul the continuing decisions of the Council: not to review within six months or thereafter Council Decision 2006/379 in relation to the applicant, to maintain until the date hereof and thereafter the applicant in a list of terrorist organisations established	Not decided yet.

			by Council Decision 2006/379 of 29 May 2006 with effect from the date of that decision notwithstanding the judgment of this Court in Case T-228/02 of 12 December 2006 and the Council's obligations under Article 233 EC. To order the defendant to pay the applicant damages amounting to EUR 1 090 000 and to pay the applicant's costs.	

The European Court of Justice

Applicant(s)	Date	Case reference	Details	Judgment
Gestoras Pro Amnistía association, Juan Mari Olano Olano and Julen Zelarain Errasti	17 August 2004	C-354/04 P	Appeal against CFI judgment in Case T-333/02, above; joined with case C-355/04 (below).	Opinion of AG recommending rejection 26 October 2006 Appeal dismissed 27 February 2007
SEGI association, Araitz Zubimendi Izaga and Aritza Galarraga	17 August 2004	C-355/04 P	Appeal against CFI judgment in Case T-338/02, above; joined with case C-354/04 (above).	Opinion of AG recommending rejection 26 October 2006 Appeal dismissed 27 February 2007
Kurdistan Workers Party	18 May 2005	C-229/05 P	Appeal against CFI judgment in Case T-	Sets aside the order of the CFI in

(PKK) and Kurdistan National Congress (KNK)			229/02, above.	so far as it dismisses the application of Osman Ocalan, dismissed the appeal as to the remainder 18 January 2007
Jose Maria Sison (access to documents cases)	27 June 2005	C-266/05 P	Appeal against CFI judgment in Cases T-110/03, T-150/03 and T-405/03, above.	Dismissed 1 February 2007
Kadi v Council and Commission	24 November 2005	C-402/05 P	Appeal against CFI judgment in Case T-315/01, above.	Not decided yet.
Yusuf and Al Barakaat International Foundation v Council	1 December 2005	C-415/05 P	Appeal against CFI judgment in Case T-315/01, above.	Not decided yet.
Gerda and Christiane Möllendorf (concerns Salem-Abdul Ghani El-Rafei, Dr. Kamal Rafehi and Agccl A. Al-Ageel)	21 February 2006	C-117/06 P	Reference from German Courts regarding sale of property by persons listed by UN Taleban Sanctions Committee.	Not decided yet.

The European Court of Human Rights

The European Court of Human Rights has held that *all* judicial remedies (including the EU Courts) must be exhausted before it can consider any cases - leaving applicants facing lengthy procedures.

See Judgment (23 May 2002) in Case Nos. 6422/02 and 9916/02, SEGI association, Gestoras Pro Amnistía and Others vs. Council of the European Union.

Source: Statewatch (2007). Updated by the author on July 2, 2007.

V. Article 9 of the Agreement on Mutual Legal Assistance between the European Union and the United States of America

Limitations on use to protect personal and other data

1. The requesting State may use any evidence or information obtained from the requested State:
(a) for the purpose of its criminal investigations and proceedings;
(b) for preventing an immediate and serious threat to its public security;
(c) in its non-criminal judicial or administrative proceedings directly related to investigations or proceedings:
(i) set forth in subparagraph (a); or
(ii) for which mutual legal assistance was rendered under Article 8;
(d) for any other purpose, if the information or evidence has been made public within the framework of proceedings for which they were transmitted, or in any of the situations described in subparagraphs (a), (b) and (c); and
(e) for any other purpose, only with the prior consent of the requested State.

2. (a) This Article shall not prejudice the ability of the requested State to impose additional conditions in a particular case where the particular request for assistance could not be complied with in the absence of such conditions. Where additional conditions have been imposed in accordance with this subparagraph, the requested State may require the requesting State to give information on the use made of the evidence or information;
(b) Generic restrictions with respect to the legal standards of the requesting State for processing personal data may not be imposed by the requested State as a condition under subparagraph (a) to providing evidence or information

3. Where, following disclosure to the requesting State, the requested State becomes aware of circumstances that may cause it to seek an additional condition in a particular case, the requested State may consult with the requesting State to determine the extent to which the evidence and information can be protected.

4. A requested State may apply the use limitation provision of the applicable bilateral mutual legal assistance treaty in lieu of this Article, where doing so will result in less restriction on the use of information and evidence than provided for in this Article.

5. Where a bilateral mutual legal assistance treaty in force between a Member State and the United States of America on the date of signature of this Agreement, permits limitation of the obligation to provide assistance with respect to certain tax offences, the Member State concerned may indicate, in its exchange of written instruments with the United States of America described in Article 3(2), that, with respect to such offences, it will continue to apply the use limitation provision of that treaty.

***ibidem*-Verlag**
Melchiorstr. 15
D-70439 Stuttgart
info@ibidem-verlag.de
www.ibidem-verlag.de
www.edition-noema.de
www.autorenbetreuung.de

Zeitfracht Medien GmbH
Ferdinand-Jühlke-Straße 7
99095 Erfurt, Deutschland
produktsicherheit@kolibri360.de